The SHEPHERD

AS

LEADER

John MacArthur

GENERAL EDITOR

HARVEST HOUSE PUBLISHERS
EUGENE, OREGON

Cover by Harvest House Publishers, Inc.

Cover photo © deathtothestockphoto.com

THE SHEPHERD AS LEADER

Copyright © 2016 Grace Community Church
Published by Harvest House Publishers
Eugene, Oregon 97402
www.harvesthousepublishers.com

Library of Congress Cataloging-in-Publication Data

The shepherd as leader / John MacArthur, general editor.
    pages cm — (The shepherd's library)
    ISBN 978-0-7369-6209-4 (hardcover)
    ISBN 978-0-7369-6210-0 (eBook)
    1. Christian leadership—Congresses. 2. Pastoral theology—Congresses. | macArthur, John, 1939- editor.
    BV652.1.S53 2016
    253—dc23   2015025423

CONTENTS

INTRODUCTION

The first Shepherds' Conference was held on March 19, 1980, at Grace Community Church, where 159 men gathered to focus on the theme of pastoral ministry. From the beginning, the goal was to live out Paul's mandate to Timothy: "The things which you have heard from me in the presence of many witnesses, entrust these to faithful men who will be able to teach others also" (2 Timothy 2:2).

What started as a small event has, by God's grace, blossomed into an international movement with thousands in attendance each spring. Over the years, pastors from every state and nearly 100 countries have come to the conference to be challenged and encouraged in areas of preaching, theology, leadership, discipleship, and counseling. My own heart has been deeply blessed by the faithful men I've met and fellowshipped with at the conference.

Since its inception, the Shepherds' Conference has featured hundreds of sermons specifically directed at pastors and church leaders. Because the truth of God's Word is timeless, those messages are still as rich and powerful today as when they were first preached. That is why I was so grateful when Harvest House Publishers approached me about publishing this second volume—a collection of the most memorable Shepherds' Conference messages on the topic of leadership.

Today more than ever, the church needs a restored model of leadership that is based on God's Word and that brings Him glory, which is why a book on this subject is so timely. The aim of this volume is to encourage pastors to fulfill their pastoral mandate: to exemplify the truest kind of leadership, which according to Christ, demands service, sacrifice, and selflessness.

This book is for all spiritual leaders, whether you've been to the Shepherds' Conference or not. As you read it, my prayer is that your passion for truth will burn brighter and your resolve for Christ's glory will grow stronger as you seek to serve and lead His church.

For the Great Shepherd,
John MacArthur

Humility: An Essential for Ministry

"Whoever receives this child in My name receives Me,
and whoever receives Me receives Him who sent Me;
for the one who is least among all of you,
this is the one who is great."

Luke 9:48

1

Humility: An Essential for Ministry

John MacArthur

Shepherds' Conference 2005

Luke 9:46–56

It is easy to be proud when we are right. Our theology is right. Our understanding of the Word of God is right. Our view of Scripture as the inerrant revelation of the holy God is right. Our understanding of the gospel is right. We have the right message to preach to the world. It is difficult to be humble when we are right, for we can become intolerant and heavy-handed. The reminder to be humble is a helpful one. The reminder to speak the truth in love and to be patient is necessary. Ironically, we live in a world that exalts self-love, self-satisfaction, self-promotion. For the world, it is considered virtuous to exalt self. But as pastors, we are forced to live in a counterculture way by being models of selfless humility in a world that sees that as a weakness.

The Perils of Pride

Children of God are commanded to be humble because Scripture sees pride as an ugly sin that the devil committed along with the other angels who joined his rebellion. Pride is the sin that led to Adam and Eve being thrown out of the Garden. It is that damning sin that produced rebellion against God and His law, for it was pride that sought to dethrone God, strike at His absolute perfect sovereignty, and replace Him with self. This kind of pride naturally grips every human heart.

Pride is the reason it is difficult to come to Christ. After all, who wants to hate and deny self? Yet Jesus taught just that message—a message that one cannot come into His kingdom if he does not hate himself. It is tough to refuse to associate any longer with the person you are—to set aside your own desires, ambitions, dreams, goals, and come empty-handed, broken, and contrite to Christ.

It wasn't too many years ago when a wide-eyed first-year seminary student asked me, "Dr. MacArthur, how did you finally overcome pride?" A genuine but silly question because no one will ever overcome pride until this fallen flesh is forsaken. Battling pride will continue until the day of glorification. However, this does not give people an excuse to hold onto their pride. Pride has to be broken for individuals to be saved, and it has to be continually broken for individuals to be sanctified.

The Pastor's Pride

My fear is that pastors who attend conferences like the Shepherds' Conference, who read the right books, and who accumulate the right knowledge may be motivated and energized to go out and fight the battle for the truth in the wrong way. I fear that well-equipped pastors are often too ready to pound on people who are slow to learn and accept certain truths. Pastor, the more you know and the more mature you are, then the more impact your ministry has, the more blessing you experience upon your life, and the more likely you are to feed your pride.

This is what the apostle Paul wrote about in 2 Corinthians when the Lord sent him a messenger of Satan; I believe that is a reference to a group of false teachers who came to Corinth and troubled the church. The chaos this group caused devastated the apostle. Paul experienced much agony as he watched a church be shredded by false teaching—a church into which he had invested so much of his life. He even prayed three times for the Lord to remove this thorn, but he recognized that the Lord had sent it to pierce his otherwise proud flesh. Paul said the reason God sent this message of Satan was to keep him from exalting himself.

**It is when you come to the end of yourself that you
experience the power of God.**

Paul had seen many revelations, had been to heaven and back, witnessed things unspeakable, was caught up to the third heaven, and had personal private appearances of the resurrected Lord Jesus Christ (2 Corinthians 12:1-7). This man had plenty to be proud of, and when the Lord needed to humble His otherwise proud servant, He sent a demon in the purposes of His providence. In the midst of this pain, Paul knew that God's grace was sufficient and that God's power would be perfected in his weakness. Beloved, it is when you come to the end of yourself that you experience the power of God.

A Lesson on Humility

In Luke chapter 9, Jesus taught a lesson on humility. At this point, the disciples had been with Jesus for more than two-and-a-half years, twenty-four hours a day, seven days a week. They were constantly in the presence of Jesus, and every location was a classroom and everything was a lesson. These followers experienced relentless teaching, and everything Jesus taught them was absolutely right. Every word Jesus spoke came from a divine mind and because of this, the disciples were taught perfectly.

In addition, the disciples were given authority to represent Jesus Christ by proclaiming the gospel of the kingdom from town to town and village to village. These men were given so much authority that if they went into a town that did not receive their message, they were to pronounce a judgment on those people, shake the dust off their feet, and leave. The disciples were also given the power to cast out demons and to heal diseases. Common, ordinary men received an immense amount of truth, authority, and divine power to wield in the name of Jesus Christ. As a result, their flesh was having a difficult time fighting pride, and it was necessary for our Lord to teach them what it meant to be humble. Jesus did exactly that in Luke chapter 9, and Jesus' class on humility applies to us as well.

In the beginning of Luke 9 we read that the disciples were given power and authority to cast out demons, heal diseases, proclaim the kingdom, pronounce judgment on cities, and shake the dust off their feet. With this power and authority they went "preaching the gospel and healing everywhere" (Luke 9:6). To add to that, Peter, John, and James were taken up to a mountain with Jesus, where He pulled aside His flesh and was transfigured (verses 28-29). On that mountain, those three disciples saw the shining glory of God and met Moses and Elijah. These men experienced an astonishing, unique, and unequaled event.

With all that they had experienced, it was difficult for the disciples to stay humble. So as they came down the mountain, they had an argument "as to which of them might be the greatest" (9:46). You can imagine what was said during that argument. One of them may have said, "Well, you never know, it could be me." And James could have responded, "Well if it was going to be you, you would have been on the mountain with us." Instantly, the group would have been narrowed to three. One might have said, "We were taken up on the mountain, you weren't." Then another may have chimed in, "In the last village we visited, how many people did you heal?" The answer would've come, "Well, I had some minor healings." The retort, "Ha! I had five major healings." One can just imagine the argument taking place between the disciples.

It is important to remember that the disciples are listed in Matthew, Mark, Luke, and Acts. In each of the lists, three groups of four disciples are mentioned. The groups appear in the order of their descending intimacy with Christ. Every time those lists are given, each disciple stays in his group, and the first name in each group never changes. This means that there were leaders over each of the groups. Peter was the first name listed in the most intimate group. He was the leader amongst the other leaders. So to put it simply, there was a pecking order. The first group was very bold. Peter was in this group along with James and John, also known as the Sons of Thunder. And because the disciples lived in a world of hierarchical understanding, they were arguing over who the greatest was by comparing all of their spiritual experiences, opportunities to display power, personal moments with Jesus, and even the incredible event on the mountain.

Evidently the argument was so intense that James and John asked their mother to go to Jesus and plead their case to sit at His right and left hands. The Sons of Thunder did this because their mother was related to Jesus' mother, and they assumed they had the inside family track. These men had the right message and were God's chosen representatives, yet they still faced the issue of pride. In this text, Jesus taught the disciples—and us—a needed lesson on humility.

Pride Ruins Unity

The first principle Jesus taught is that pride ruins unity. Luke wrote, "An argument started among them" (9:46). The Greek word translated "argument" entails a battle in which unity is fractured. The disciples were a team, and they were not supposed to be competing with one another. This first generation of gospel preachers needed to give their lives for Christ and yield their hearts to one another. Instead, they were destroying their unity in the midst of a crucial mission. Pride is capable of destroying the most intimate kind of unity. Even Jesus, while on the verge of suffering on the cross, spoke to the disciples about His own personal suffering yet could not hold their attention because they were too busy alienating one another with their desire for personal glory. Pride has the capability of destroying relationships.

For example, pride destroyed relationships between the believers in Corinth. In 2 Corinthians 12:20, Paul wrote that he feared a visit to their church because he was concerned that he would find among them strife, jealousy, anger, disputes, slander, gossip, arrogance, and disturbances. He did not know if he could handle the factions that had stemmed from pride.

Pride is capable of causing much harm, and that is why Paul wrote in Philippians 1:27 that believers were to be "striving together for the faith of the gospel." He urged the Philippians to not compete with one another but to maintain unity:

> If there is any encouragement in Christ, if there is any consola-
> tion of love, if there is any fellowship of the Spirit, if any affec-
> tion and compassion, make my joy complete by being of the
> same mind, maintaining the same love, united in spirit, intent

on one purpose. Do nothing from selfishness or empty conceit, but with humility of mind regard one another as more important than yourselves; do not merely look out for your own personal interests, but also for the interests of others. Have this attitude in yourselves which was also in Christ Jesus, who, although He existed in the form of God, did not regard equality with God a thing to be grasped, but emptied Himself, taking the form of a bond-servant, and being made in the likeness of men. Being found in appearance as a man, He humbled Himself by becoming obedient to the point of death, even death on a cross (2:1–8).

As a pastor you can preach on the topic of unity until you are blue in the face, but as long as pride exists in the church, it will continue to destroy relationships.

Pride Raises Relativity

The second principle Jesus taught is that pride raises relativity. The essence of the argument is to determine who is comparatively greater. Pride desires superiority over others, seeks to elevate itself, and compares itself with everyone else. That is exactly what Jesus accused the Pharisees of doing. These leaders loved to be noticed by men, loved the place of honor at banquets, loved the chief seats in the synagogues, loved respectful greetings in the marketplace, and loved to be called rabbi. A proud heart is incessantly fighting for the top and raising relativity by comparing itself with others. However, Jesus had and continues to have a different definition of greatness: "Everyone who exalts himself will be humbled, and he who humbles himself will be exalted" (Luke 14:11).

Pride Reveals Depravity

A third principle Jesus taught is that pride reveals sin and depravity. Luke wrote that Jesus knew "what they were thinking in their heart" (9:47). Jesus always knows what is in the heart of a person. How would you like to spend three years with God constantly reading your thoughts? That may be the greatest evidence of God's grace in using imperfect vessels. Though He knows all our thoughts, He still utilizes fallible and weak people.

No matter how much you may try to avoid creating disunity or some sort of spiritual pecking order, given enough time, the sins of the heart will still come out. Time and truth go hand in hand. A proud pastor may keep his pride under wraps for a while, but eventually the congregation will find out that he is driven by a proud heart. That is one of the main reasons some pastors have a short ministry.

The Lord, in His response, was not reacting only because of the damage pride causes, nor because of the relativity that occurs, but because of its sinfulness. Jesus knew what the disciples were thinking in their hearts as He "took a child and stood him by His side" (9:47). It was a child small enough to hold (see Mark 9:36), and yet grown enough to stand up before Jesus. This image depicts a person who comes to the Lord with no achievements, no accomplishments, and void of any self-worth. God does not care how many degrees you have, how widely you've read, how clever you are in communication, or how strong a leader you are. The only way you can approach Him is as a meek and humble child.

In that culture, children were considered the weakest, most ignored, and most vulnerable of all people. They were viewed as having little value, and many of them didn't survive to become adults. Jesus used this little child to teach the disciples that they were viewing themselves as kings when they were acting like children. The sin of pride fails to recognize the complete and utter dependence on God that a person needs to have. Pride reveals sin and depravity.

Pride Rejects Deity

Fourth, pride rejects deity. Jesus said in Luke 9:48, "Whoever receives this child in My name receives Me, and whoever receives Me receives Him who sent Me." The child is representative of those who are Jesus' disciples. Jesus made it clear that unless one becomes like a child, he will not enter the kingdom. Therefore, those who reject Christ reject the presence of God in other believers. These children of God are precious to the Lord, and they must be precious to us as well.

As pastors, may we never say that we do not have time for other Christians, because the Holy Spirit dwells in every believer. The disciples felt that Jesus was wasting His time by interacting with children, but note

His response to them: "Permit the children to come to Me; do not hinder them, for the kingdom of God belongs to such as these" (Mark 10:14). We must be very careful when it comes to rejecting, offending, or belittling other believers, because when we do, we're offending Christ, who dwells in them. Pride thinks it's better than another believer in whom Christ dwells, and thus pride rejects deity.

Pride Reverses Reality

The fifth principle Jesus taught is that pride reverses reality. "The one who is least among all of you, this is the one who is great" (Luke 9:48). This truth upsets the world and overturns conventional wisdom. Worldly wisdom claims that whoever is the most popular, the most widely known, the most influential, and the most powerful is the greatest. Pride attempts to reverse the reality that it's the servant who is the greatest. Paul stressed this truth in 1 Corinthians 1:26-28 when he wrote about the Lord establishing His church with not many noble, not many mighty, but instead the lowly, the base, and the weak. He did this so that the glory might be His and that there would be no other explanation for the existence of the church other than the purposes of God.

Beloved, we are the lowly and the least. Our battle should focus on seeing who can serve the most, because "whoever wishes to become great among you shall be your servant" (Matthew 20:26). Pride attempts to reverse reality, and this is seen even in the Christian world. People who are honored, popular, and have accomplished all kinds of things tend to become relentlessly self-promoting. As ministers of God, this is a battle we have to fight, and we are to strive to be lowly like Jesus.

Pride Reacts with Exclusivity

Sixth, pride reacts with exclusivity. For this lesson we look at Luke 9:49: "John answered and said, 'Master, we saw someone casting out demons in Your name; and we tried to prevent him because he does not follow along with us.'" Here we see John reacting with exclusivity. John was a dynamic, driven man; he was not meek. What did not help was that he had just come down from the mountain of transfiguration. It is in the midst of all this that John came across someone casting out demons in the name of Jesus Christ, and John attempted to hinder him because that person was not one of the disciples who followed Jesus. John basically said, "Hey, you're not in our group. You don't wear our label."

We read that this individual not only tried to cast out demons, he was casting them out in the name of Jesus. Maybe he was one of the seventy who were sent out, but he was not a part of the Twelve. To be doing something in Jesus' name indicates consistency with Jesus' identity and mission. Apparently this individual was a believer, though not an apostle, and he was serving for the glory of Christ. The original Greek text indicates that the man kept doing what he was doing, and John and some others were trailing along, trying to stop him. They did this because he wasn't in the group.

Pride is always sectarian and narrow. This man was not an unbeliever like Simon Magus, who was trying to buy the Holy Spirit's power (Acts 8:18-19). However, he was not directly affiliated with Jesus' group of disciples, and John had a problem with that.

I sometimes get questioned why I associate with a specific organization or person, and why they associate with me. If I were to limit my associations only to people in my group, then the world would be a lonely place. Pride wants to do exactly that. Pride says, "I know more than you. I don't know if I can work with you. You need correction. You need help. You're not quite there. Once you get there, then I'll work with you." Humility says, "If you're doing this in the name of Christ and doing your best to serve Christ, I'll come alongside you," because there is latitude and generosity among the humble.

Jesus made it clear that there is no middle ground. If someone is for Christ and is doing his best to serve Christ, then stop trying to hinder him. Jesus replied to John, "Do not hinder him; for he who is not against you is for you" (Luke 9:50). The true church is a very diverse place. I have been all over the world, and it is evident that cultures, styles, and expressions of worship vary from region to region. Though I might do certain things differently, if they are for Christ, then I am called to not hinder that effort. But it's difficult to be humble when you think you're right. We must humble ourselves and realize that we are all still in-process.

> Humility belongs to those who understand that the
> way down is the way up.

Humility pursues unity by seeking to exalt others. Humility refuses relative comparisons. Humility purifies the inner person of all selfishness. Humility belongs to those who exalt God alone as the object of worship, and recognizes that they should not reject fellow believers, but honor and love them. Humility belongs to those who understand that the way down is the way up. Humility is characteristic of those who embrace the diversity of true believers.

Pride Restrains Mercy

The seventh and final principle Jesus taught is that pride restrains mercy. As we approach the end of Luke 9, we read that the Galilean ministry has ended and the days were approaching for Jesus' ascension to Jerusalem and ultimately the cross (verse 51). The scene changes, but the lesson on humility continues, and here we find an illustration of how pride restrains mercy. To show mercy is to be generous, kind, and selfless. The opposite is a lack of mercy, which is reserved for the rankest kind of people—those filled with vengeance, vitriol, and viciousness. On this occasion, we read that some of the disciples were merciless: "He sent messengers on ahead of Him, and they went and entered a village of the Samaritans to make arrangements for Him. But they did not receive Him, because He was traveling toward Jerusalem. When His disciples James and John saw this, they said, 'Lord, do You want us to command fire to come down from heaven and consume them?'" (Luke 9:52-54).

The Samaritans were a mixed race of Semite pagans left over from the Northern Kingdom. After the Northern Kingdom was invaded by the Assyrians, the people who were left intermarried with pagans and became loyal to the Assyrian king. They were hated by the Jews because they were considered to be half-breeds who had rejected their race and their faith.

While the Jews rejected the Samaritans, Jesus did not. In John 4, we read about ministering to these people because the gospel was intended for the Gentiles too. So in Luke 9, Jesus visited a Samaritan village to preach the kingdom. As He approached, Jesus sent out messengers to make preparations. However, the townspeople rejected Jesus and prevented Him from coming. They refused Him because He was journeying with His face toward Jerusalem, and they despised the Jews. Because the Samaritans were not allowed to worship in Jerusalem, they had to build their own place of worship at Gerazim. To make matters worse, in 128 BC, their temple at Gerazim was destroyed. This made them hate the Jews even more.

When James and John saw this rejection, they asked the Lord, "Do You want us to command fire to come down from heaven and consume them?" Well, that's a strange reaction to unbelief. They didn't show a missionary heart. And when did these disciples ever have the ability to express such a power? Where did they get that idea? Remember that they had just been with Elijah at the transfiguration, and most likely they were recalling an incident that is recorded in 2 Kings 1.

There, we read that Ahaziah, the king of the Northern Kingdom, sent 50 men along with a captain to take Elijah prisoner. When the captain saw Elijah, he said, "O man of God, the king says, 'Come down'" (verse 9), which was another way of saying, "You're under arrest." Elijah answered, "If I am a man of God, let fire come down from heaven and consume you and your fifty" (verse 10). And fire came down from heaven, and consumed the men. The foolish king sent another group of men, and the captain of this group said, "O man of God, thus says the king, 'Come down quickly'" (verse 11). Elijah answered, "If I am a man of God, let fire come down from heaven and consume you and your fifty" (verse 12). Once again the fire of God came down from heaven, and this group was consumed.

The king sent a third group. At least this captain was rational—he came before Elijah, bowed on his knees, and pleaded, "O man of God, please let my life and the lives of these fifty servants of yours be precious in your sight" (verse 13). He continued, "Behold fire came down from heaven and consumed the first two captains of fifty with their fifties: but now let my life be precious in your sight" (verse 14). As a result, the angel of the Lord said to Elijah:

"Go down with him; do not be afraid of him." So he arose and went down with him to the king. Then he said to him, "Thus says the LORD, 'Because you have sent messengers to inquire of Baal-zebub, the god of Ekron—is it because there is no God in Israel to inquire of His word?—therefore you shall not come down from the bed where you have gone up, but shall surely die'" (verses 15-16).

We learn in verse 17 that the king died "according to the word of the LORD."

Going back to Luke 9, the disciples remembered what Elijah had done and wanted to call fire down from heaven as well. Instead of receiving confirmation, however, the disciples received a rebuke from the Lord: "He turned and rebuked them, and said, 'You do not know what kind of spirit you are of; for the Son of Man did not come to destroy men's lives, but to save them.' And they went on to another village" (verses 55-56).

Jesus was on a mission of mercy, but the disciples' pride restrained their mercy. We can never turn the opponents of the gospel into the enemy. If we attack everyone who disagrees with us by labeling them, assaulting them, and calling them names, then we are distancing the mission field from ourselves. The lost are not the enemy; they are the mission field. The fire will come one day, but until that day, we are commissioned to participate in a mission of mercy.

That little Samaritan village was saved from physical fire. And later we read in Acts 8 that Philip, a deacon in the early church, preached in Samaria. Perhaps many of the Samaritans were also saved from the eternal flame by Philip's preaching.

As pastors, we are on a mission of mercy, and we cannot alienate the very people we are called to reach. Yet pride will do just that because pride restrains mercy. We know the truth, and we have the truth. But we should not let this knowledge make us proud; rather, we are to preach the truth with love and humility. Jesus said, "Be merciful as your Father in heaven is merciful. And be humble, as Christ who humbled himself."

PRAYER

Father, Your Word is precious. Your Word is rich. Your Word is powerful. May we learn well these principles on humility. Jesus could have brought down fire from heaven, but instead, He just went to another place. Help us manifest all the characteristics of humility and none of the ugly characteristics of pride. We commend ourselves again to Your grace and to Your Word, which is able to build us up and give an inheritance to us, which we wait for with joy. In Christ's name, Amen.

Purity in the Camp

"The priest shall then write these curses on a scroll,
and he shall wash them off into the water of bitterness."

Numbers 5:23

2

Purity in the Camp

Ligon Duncan
Shepherds' Conference 2007

Numbers 5:11-31

For the last eight years, I have consecutively preached my way through a book of the Pentateuch on Sunday mornings, followed by a book of the Psalms on Sunday evenings.

While preaching through the Pentateuch, I dreaded coming to the book of Numbers. My friend John Currid, who is in the midst of writing a commentary on the whole of the Pentateuch, wrote on the books in this order: Genesis, Exodus, Leviticus, Deuteronomy, and then he went back to Numbers. So even a scholar of the Old Testament like John Currid approached the book of Numbers with some fear and trepidation.

Numbers may well not be your favorite book in the Bible, and perhaps you are not particularly excited about learning from it. You might not have read the book in a long time, much less preached a sermon from it. The book consists of 36 chapters, 1288 verses, laws, sand, desert, grumbling, and wandering. Doesn't sound too hopeful, does it?

But I want you to see how important, exciting, practical, and applicable the book of Numbers is. Yet at the same time, there are some challenges facing us when we come to it.

Challenges to the Book of Numbers

A Book of History

For one thing, Numbers is a book of history, and in the modern world, we dislike history because we don't know much about it. At the beginning of the twentieth century, Henry Ford taught us that history is bunk. We rarely think that the events that happened 20 years ago have anything to do with today, and if they do, we still choose to not remember them. One British scholar, Ambrose Bierce, said, with tongue firmly planted in cheek, that "war is God's way of teaching Americans geography."[1]

I would add history to that statement as well.

Like it or not, the Book that we preach is a book of history. Even if you don't love history, biblical history is like none you've ever read. Californians will remember their former governor, Ronald Reagan, who was capable of telling history through stories that would draw you into the experience. Moses was able to do that as well. He told history in such a way that he planted you into the middle of the story. He made you realize that these are your people; this is your story. I grew up in the Deep South. My father used to take me to graveyards and say, "Son, these are your people." (Trust me when I say Southerners are strange.) Moses, from 3400 years ago, was saying to us, "These are your people. Learn from them."

A Book of Disobedience

Another challenge to teaching, preaching, and learning from the book of Numbers is that it's filled with stories about people behaving terribly. Who wants to hear about that? Instead, let's be positive, optimistic, upbeat, and hopeful about human nature. But we're pastors. Like our Master, we have not been called to the righteous, but to sinners. Even in our churches there are individuals still battling with indwelling sin. Individuals who, by the powerful operation of the Holy Spirit, have been called to faith in Christ and united with Him. Individuals who have been gloriously converted from the inside out by that sovereign regenerating work of the Holy Spirit, yet still struggle with sin.

The pastor's life consists of dealing with people behaving badly. What better book to go to than Numbers? We are just like the Israelites, and though we'd rather not think about our sin, it is so important that we do.

We need to think about it, we need to own it, we need to see its danger and its consequences, and we need to repent and deal with it. Numbers will help us do that.

A Book Uniquely Organized

Third, this book is filled with stories, and the flow of these stories is sometimes interrupted by what seem like arbitrary sections of laws and bizarre procedures. Moses was not only a great storyteller, he was also an excellent organizer. You will find that the story sections of this book are related to the law sections of this book. And the law sections are related to the procedure sections. There is an underlying logic to it all. Of course, Moses had a great ghostwriter: God, the Holy Spirit, authored these words. And once you understand the logic of the organization, you appreciate the book all the more because of the different ways that Moses drove home the truth.

Nine Things Paul Said About Numbers

Just in case you're not yet convinced of the importance of studying Numbers, I want to take you to the New Testament—to the apostle Paul and 1 Corinthians 10. After that, I want to look at a hymn that we all know and love. All this is to try to convince you of how applicable, helpful, important, and edifying Numbers is.

Look with me at 1 Corinthians 10:1-13. Everything that Paul talked about in this passage happened in the wilderness and was recorded by Moses in either Exodus or Numbers. The key point that the apostle wanted to make to the Christians in Corinth comes right out of the book of Numbers. Paul was saying how Numbers is important, helpful, applicable, and edifying. But he said more than that—he was telling us that the book of Numbers was written for us. He said that the events recorded in Numbers happened for our benefit, and that God wants us to learn from them how we are to live today.

Let's look at what Paul wrote:

> I do not want you to be unaware, brethren, that our fathers were all under the cloud and all passed through the sea; and all were baptized into Moses in the cloud and in the sea; and

all ate the same spiritual food; and all drank the same spiritual drink, for they were drinking from a spiritual rock which followed them; and the rock was Christ. Nevertheless, with most of them God was not well-pleased; for they were laid low in the wilderness.

Now these things happened as examples for us, so that we would not crave evil things as they also craved. Do not be idolaters, as some of them were; as it is written, "The people sat down to eat and drink, and stood up to play." Nor let us act immorally, as some of them did, and twenty-three thousand fell in one day. Nor let us try the Lord, as some of them did, and were destroyed by the serpents. Nor grumble, as some of them did, and were destroyed by the destroyer. Now these things happened to them as an example, and they were written for our instruction, upon whom the ends of the ages have come. Therefore let him who thinks he stands take heed that he does not fall. No temptation has overtaken you but such as is common to man; and God is faithful, who will not allow you to be tempted beyond what you are able, but with the temptation will provide the way of escape also, so that you will be able to endure it.

I want you to notice nine things in this passage that the apostle Paul said about the book of Numbers.

Our focus should be on the redeeming work of Christ and how that particular story contributes to the development of that grand biblical theme.

First, notice Paul wrote that the events that occurred in the wilderness serve as examples "for our instruction." It's very popular today, in some circles, to say, "All our preaching must be redemptive historical," in the sense that it only draws attention to the big picture of God's redeeming purposes in any particular passage. This view endorses that there should be no application and we should never preach examples from the Old Testament because that's moralism. Instead, our focus should be on the redeeming work of Christ and how that particular story contributes to the development of that grand biblical theme.

There are many helpful things emphasized by those who are interested in promoting redemptive historical preaching, and it is a helpful corrective to non-cross-centered, non-gospel-centered exposition. But it has a slight problem, and that problem is with the New Testament. The New Testament uses examples from the Old Testament and applies them to Christians, both negatively and positively. That's exactly what the apostle Paul was doing in 1 Corinthians 10:1-13. He was referencing what the children of Israel did in the wilderness, as recorded in Numbers, and he wrote to the Corinthians and to us and said, "See what they did? Don't do that."

Jesus did the same thing when He turned to His disciples and said, "Remember Lot's wife" (Luke 17:32). James did the same and gave a positive example when he said, "I have to get these guys to pray like Christians. Let's see what illustration could I use…Elijah! Pray like Elijah. There was a drought in the land until that man started praying, and God sent down rain. That's how you pray, Christians—like Elijah" (see James 5:16-18).

The New Testament is filled with examples of the inspired writers of Scripture using the Old Testament to encourage and to exhort believers to live the Christian life. That's what Paul was doing in 1 Corinthians 10— he said the events that occurred in the wilderness occurred as examples for us (verses 5-6).

Second, notice Paul said that the events that occurred in the wilderness were designed to provide a moral warning to us. Look at verse 6: "Now these things happened as examples for us, so that we would not crave evil things as they also craved." Those events served as moral exhortations designed to warn us about the danger of sin.

Third, notice again in verse 6 that the apostle did not simply say these things were recorded as examples for us. He wrote, "These things *happened* as examples for us." Our breath ought to be taken away by this; men lost their wives, women lost their husbands, parents lost their children, children lost their parents and their grandparents in the desert. Paul was in no way belittling the experiences of the people of God in the wilderness. But he made it clear that, in God's design, this happened in order that He could give an example to you. That is how much God loves you, and that is how much He cares for you. He does not waste life, for He created it. He does not treat the lives of His people flippantly and glibly, and yet the lives of thousands and thousands of people were affected in the course of His providence. The apostle Paul said, "This happened for you." All the more that we should say, "Those are my people."

Fourth, the events of Numbers provide exhortation to Christians. Look at verse 7: "Do not be idolaters, as some of them were." Then look at verse 11: "Now these things happened to them as an example, and they were written for our instruction, upon whom the ends of the ages have come." God, in His providence, has in view New Covenant believers in the events recorded in the book of Numbers.

Fifth, notice that Paul specifically applied these exhortations to New Testament believers in four areas. One, "do not be idolaters" (verse 7). The whole Bible was written as a full-scale assault on idolatry. The first thing that Paul wanted us to learn from Numbers is not to be idolaters. You can't imagine how crucial this is for life in the Christian congregation. If we're going to be disciples, and not just a bunch of people who merely sit on the pew, we must be committed to the worship of the one true God in all of life. That means not being idolaters.

Two, Paul declared from the story of the Israelites in the wilderness that we are not to be immoral. Many people under the assault of our toxic culture are beginning to think, *We've been too narrow on moral issues, and the Christian church ought to be big enough to handle the various types of sexual diversities that exist in our culture.* Contrary to that, the apostle Paul wrote in verse 8, "Nor let us act immorally, as some of them did, and twenty-three thousand fell in one day."

Three, notice Paul wrote that we're not to presumptuously test the Lord like Israel did.

And four, we're not to grumble against providence like they did (verses 7-10). Those are the specific ways Paul applied moral exhortation to New Testament believers.

Sixth, not only did these events happen for Christians, but we're told in verse 11 that they were *written down* for Christians. God intentionally had these events recorded for us: "Now these things happened to them as an example, and they were written down for our instruction, upon whom the ends of the ages have come." The inscripturation of this story had in view a benefit to God's New Covenant people.

Seventh, the apostle Paul warned us in this text against thinking that we will not fall like the Israelites did. "Don't think, New Covenant Christian," he was saying, "that just because you have seen the glories of the cross that you are impervious to the temptation to fall like the children of Israel in the wilderness" (paraphrase).

Eighth, we are to learn from the Israelites' temptations and failures in order to escape our own (verse 13). You've heard the platitude that he who does not learn from history is doomed to repeat it. Well, this is the spiritual corollary to that platitude: "Look at their failures. Look at their temptations and escape yours, Christian."

Then *ninth*, the apostle Paul said that Christ is right at the center of this whole wilderness account (verse 4). He's the rock that followed the people. This is all about exalting Christ.

Hymnal Support

Now, if Paul hasn't convinced you, let me ask you to consider a song found in hymnals. William Williams, the greatest of the Welsh Christian poets, wrote a hymn called "Guide Me, O Thou Great Jehovah." That hymn is the book of Numbers applied to Christians. If you've sung that song before, you've been singing about Numbers being applied to modern-day believers. "Guide Me, O Thou Great Jehovah" is William Williams' Christian meditation on the story that is recorded in Numbers.

Introducing Numbers 5

I hope by now you are seeing that Numbers is a glorious, profitable, applicable, and exciting book to study. Now we turn to Numbers 5. This chapter can be outlined into three parts: Verses 1 to 4 recount physical impurities that can defile you and require you to be removed from the camp. Verses 5 to 10 recount certain moral offenses that can defile you and require you to be removed from the camp. And verses 11 to 31 deal with domestic tensions eventuated either by marital infidelity or the fear of it. These sections are grouped in this chapter and have to do with issues that defile the camp.

The first five chapters of Numbers discuss how to live with God in your midst. He is holy, and there are certain requirements for His people to meet so they can be holy as He is. Therefore, chapter 5 is essential because it clarifies what defiles the camp and dishonors God. Consequently, the Israelites were to deal with defiled people with the utmost seriousness.

Numbers 5:1-10 immediately reveals the practical significance of separation from the defiled. The listed physical impurities were a potential danger to the camp, literally to their lives.

There were no antibiotics back then, which meant disease could spread like wildfire through the camp. Coming into contact with the dead and the bacteria that they carried, or a person with a blood disease and the bacteria that he or she carried, or a leper and the dangerous infections that lepers carried could be detrimental to the community. There are obvious reasons why you would want to isolate people with such physical impurities from the camp.

Of course, there is also an obvious theological reason that such separation was to be done. This whole passage is teaching us what God is like. In this context, the emphasis is that God is holy and He is present. Because He is holy and He is present, we must meet certain requirements if we are going to dwell near Him. The laws themselves are God-centered. They point us to Him. They teach us about whom He is and what He has done.

That portion of the chapter is basically self-explanatory. Next, I want to draw your attention to what appears to be a bizarre and seemingly inapplicable section that looks at strained marital relations. Look with me at verses 11 to 31:

> Then the LORD spoke to Moses, saying, "Speak to the sons of Israel and say to them, 'If any man's wife goes astray and is unfaithful to him, and a man has intercourse with her and it is hidden from the eyes of her husband and she is undetected, although she has defiled herself, and there is no witness against

her and she has not been caught in the act, if a spirit of jealousy comes over him and he is jealous of his wife when she has defiled herself, or if a spirit of jealousy comes over him and he is jealous of his wife when she has not defiled herself, the man shall then bring his wife to the priest, and shall bring as an offering for her one-tenth of an ephah of barley meal; he shall not pour oil on it nor put frankincense on it, for it is a grain offering of jealousy, a grain offering of memorial, a reminder of iniquity.

'Then the priest shall bring her near and have her stand before the LORD, and the priest shall take holy water in an earthenware vessel; and he shall take some of the dust that is on the floor of the tabernacle and put it into the water. The priest shall then have the woman stand before the LORD and let the hair of the woman's head go loose, and place the grain offering of memorial in her hands, which is the grain offering of jealousy, and in the hand of the priest is to be the water of bitterness that brings a curse. The priest shall have her take an oath and shall say to the woman, "If no man has lain with you and if you have not gone astray into uncleanness, being under the authority of your husband, be immune to this water of bitterness that brings a curse; if you, however, have gone astray, being under the authority of your husband, and if you have defiled yourself and a man other than your husband has had intercourse with you" (then the priest shall have the woman swear with the oath of the curse, and the priest shall say to the woman), "the LORD make you a curse and an oath among your people by the LORD is making your thigh waste away and your abdomen swell; and this water that brings a curse shall go into your stomach, and make your abdomen swell and your thigh waste away." And the woman shall say, "Amen. Amen."

'The priest shall then write these curses on a scroll, and he shall wash them off into the water of bitterness. Then he shall make the woman drink the water of bitterness that brings a curse, so that the water which brings a curse will go into her and cause bitterness. The priest shall take the grain offering of jealousy from the woman's hand, and he shall wave the grain offering before the LORD and bring it to the altar; and the priest shall take a handful of the grain offering as its memorial offering and offer it up in smoke on the altar, and afterward he shall make the woman drink the water. When he has made her drink the water, then it shall come about, if she has defiled herself and has been unfaithful to her husband, that the water which brings a curse will go into her and cause bitterness, and her abdomen will swell and her thigh will waste away, and the woman will become a curse among her people. But if the woman has not defiled herself and is clean, she will then be free and conceive children.

'This is the law of jealousy: when a wife, being under the authority of her husband, goes astray and defiles herself, or when a spirit of jealousy comes over a man and he is jealous of his wife, he shall then make the woman stand before the LORD, and the priest shall apply all this law to her. Moreover, the man will be free from guilt, but that woman shall bear her guilt.'"

Learning from Numbers 5

There are five things we should note in this passage. *First*, we should see the larger theological significance of this ritual because it seems bizarre at first glance. It may even appear to be chauvinistic. *Second*, we should observe what this ritual teaches us about the importance of sexual purity for all of the people of God. Sexual purity is not just an issue about you individually. It's not just an issue about you and your relationship with God. It is an issue that impacts the whole of the people of God. *Third*, we need to see what this ritual teaches us about the appointed ordinances of God in Scripture, and even about baptism and the Lord's Supper. *Fourth*, we should see what this ritual teaches us about the importance of the marriage bond and how that relates to us as the people of God. And *fifth*, we should note what this ritual teaches about the work of Christ on the cross.

Let me say all that in another way for sake of clarity: *One*, see the big picture. *Two*, see why it is that sexual purity matters to all the people of God. *Three*, see this passage as a pictured oath. *Four*, see what this passage has to say about the sacredness of marriage. And *five*, see what it has to say about the atoning work of Christ.

The Big Picture

First, it is important to understand the primary purpose of this text. You don't have to know much about the ancient Near East to know that the trial described here is not wholly different from the trials of ordeal that are often found in other cultures. In the ancient world, when crimes committed could not be proven, trials of ordeal were used to reveal either the guilt or the innocence of the person who was suspected of the crime.

Now, that is where the similarity ends, and the differences found in this passage point us to the fact that God's ways are just and wise even when they're seemingly unfathomable to the finite mind. For instance, we learn from the Mauryan laws and from other cultural artifacts that in the ancient world you were assumed guilty until you were proven innocent. Furthermore, cruel tests were often used in these trials of ordeal. For example, suspected adulteresses would be told to submerge one hand into a pot of boiling water. If they removed it unscathed, they were considered innocent. Sometimes suspects were forced to grasp a red-hot rod. If they released that rod from their hand and there was still flesh on their hand, rather than clinging to the rod, then they were innocent.

However, in Numbers 5 we see something entirely different. We notice how this whole test is dependent upon the effectual working of the Word of God. There is no magic here. There are no cruel trials. Instead, this trial assumes that the Word of God is effective, and that it can search out even the deep things of the heart.

The Word of God, in this case, is literally drunk by this woman, and the Word's judgment will find her out. By contrast, this test, unlike other trials of ordeal in the ancient Middle East, was physically safe. It was probably unpleasant to drink water with dust in it, but there was nothing physically harmful about ingesting it. It's important to remember that this process was controlled and was public.

> You cannot love God and live like a pagan. Instead,
> you must love God and live like a disciple.

So the big picture is that God's version of a trial of ordeal is just and wise, though it may seem unusual to our culture. But the question that should still be lingering in your mind is, "Why is this text here?" The answer is very simple and straightforward and drawn from the passage: Because adultery defiles, and thus pollutes the camp. If leprosy defiles the camp, if hemorrhages defile the camp, if dead bodies defile the camp, then adultery also defiles His camp. It is God's way of saying belief and behavior go together, truth and practice go together, and faith and life go together. You cannot love God and live like a pagan. Instead, you must love God and live like a disciple.

This whole passage presses on God's great concern for a consistent discipleship amongst His people—a consistent discipleship where heart, profession, and life are connected.

Sexual Purity Matters

Second, this passage makes it clear that sexual purity matters to the whole people of God, including your individual sexual purity and mine. Isn't it interesting that this aggrieved or suspicious man is not allowed to take matters into his own hands, no matter what the temperature of his jealousy is? Instead, he is forced to go to the priest. Do you hear an echo of that in Jesus' teaching, "Tell it to the church" (see Matthew 18:15-20)? And the Westminster Confession, the Baptist Confession of 1689, and the Savoy Confession, when it comes to issues of adultery and divorce, stress that individuals must not be left up to their own consciences, but must bring their concerns to the church. Moses, in Numbers, was teaching the people of God that sexual immorality is a spiritual issue, and it affects all the people of God. Your individual sexual immorality or even unwarranted jealousy is a matter that impacts the whole people of God.

You may be asking here, "Why is there a law only for a jealous husband? Isn't that a little chauvinistic?" I have three answers for you. *First,*

I don't know. In fact, we don't even know whether this law—from what we learned in the rest of the Old Testament—was ever used. There is no record of it anywhere else in the Old Testament. So, I don't know why the law was given only for jealous husbands and not jealous wives.

But *second*, this does not mean that God's law was chauvinistically tilted toward husbands, because the laws regarding adultery extended to both the husband and the wife. Moses had already covered that both a husband and a wife who committed infidelity were under the death penalty. So, it's not as if God has left husbands off the hook and put poor, defenseless women on the hook.

In fact, *third*, there may well be a logic here that is designed to protect a wife who is unjustly suspected of infidelity. In other cultures around the world, even today, if the husband is jealous of his wife, she just disappears. The chief in the village isn't consulted and the husband takes matters into his own hands. In this passage, the husband is not allowed to do that; he must bring the suspected wife to the priest. Furthermore, if this publicly embarrassing exercise can't convince a husband that his wife is innocent, nothing will. Men tend to be tempted to ungodly jealousy in a way that wives are not, and therefore God, in His wisdom and providence, provided a safe way for the people of Israel to deal with ungodly temptation.

This text teaches that sexual immorality is a spiritual issue, and unwarranted jealousy over suspected sexual immorality is a spiritual issue. And both are matters that affect the whole of the people of God.

A Pictured Oath

Third, we have a self-maledictory oath—an oath in which you call down curses, destruction, and judgment on yourself, as pictured through the actions of this ritual. Notice in verse 17 that the suspected wife must drink the holy water that contains dust from the tabernacle floor. It's important to remember that the dust from the tabernacle floor had been close to the Mercy Seat, which was the visible and tangible expression of God's presence with His people. The dust came off of holy ground. But remember too that the recipients of the five books of Moses were the children of Israel, who had in the back of their minds a story about a serpent who once had to lick the dust. They remembered their own forebearers, some of their own parents, even some of themselves who were there that day the children of Israel had to drink the dust of a golden calf. The woman suspected of adultery had to take into her body holy things that had been close to the Ark of the Covenant—things that would serve as a reminder of the judgment of God.

According to verse 18, the suspected woman had to hold an offering to the Lord in her hands as the oath was administered. It may be helpful to remember Jesus saying, "Therefore if you are presenting your offering at the altar, and there remember that your brother has something against you, leave your offering there before the altar and go; first be reconciled to your brother, and then come and present your offering" (Matthew 5:23-26). The point of Jesus' teaching is to not be a hypocrite while making the offering. Therefore, for the suspected woman to give an offering would press home to her, "If you do this and you're guilty, you are a hypocrite worshipping in the house of God. May God's curses come down upon you."

Now, pastorally speaking, understand that every component of this ritual presses home upon the woman the importance of being truthful and repentant if guilty. This is God's kindness on display! He knows that our sin is deceitful and it will hide in the smallest corners of our hearts; it never wants to be publicly revealed. As a result, God constructed a ritual that would aggressively pursue that sin and give every opportunity for that person to admit that sin and the need for grace and repentance.

Essentially what we have here is a picture of an oath. This woman is acting out a picture, the word curses of God. This is what is at work, in a positive direction, in the ordinances of baptism and the Lord's Table. The waters of baptism remind us of our union with Christ through the work of the Holy Spirit. The Lord's Table reminds us that we are invited to slide our knees up under the table of God and fellowship with Him, in Christ alone. Just as in Numbers 5 we have a picture of a curse, so in baptism and the Lord's Table we have pictures of promise.

The Sacredness of Marriage

Fourth, Numbers 5 affirms for us the sacredness of marriage. These public measures highlight the importance of marriage. They also reveal that marital fidelity is a spiritual issue that impacts the whole community and our relationship with God. Moses' point was that marital infidelity is incompatible with membership in the people of God. The New Testament presses this idea home when it tells us that marriage is a picture of the gospel. It is a picture of union with Christ. It is a picture of the relationship, which is obtained by grace, between God and His people, and therefore, for the gospel's sake, we must live out the gospel in marriage. That's why Peter told husbands who are not dealing with their wives rightly, "Your prayers will be hindered"—because marriage is a picture of the gospel (see 1 Peter 3:7).

I say this especially to these who are leaders of God's church: What's at stake in your marriage? The gospel! If your relationship with your wife—though you love Christ, she loves Christ, and you love to serve His people—is not right, then it must be your priority to make it right because it is your greatest gospel opportunity. If you neglect your marriage, then it doesn't matter what else you do because marriage matters to the gospel, to the people of God, and especially to the marriages of those whom we shepherd. One of Paul's qualifications for an elder is that he should be a man of one wife and a good leader of his household (1 Timothy 3:2-5). That logic goes all the way back to Numbers.

It's not surprising, then, that the apostle Paul wrote in 1 Corinthians that those who are unfaithful to their spouses have no place amongst the people of God (6:12-20). Or that John, in the book of Revelation, told us that there will be no immoral people in the kingdom (Revelation 22:15). This, however, does not mean that sexual infidelity is the unpardonable sin. What it does mean is that it is absolutely serious and strikes at the very heart of the gospel. It means that the only way out is a tangible repentance that expresses itself in a changed life.

The Work of Christ

Fifth, Numbers 5 points us to the atoning work of Christ. No Christian can read about the drinking of these curses without being reminded of another who drank the curse. Look at verses 23-24: "The priest shall then write these curses on a scroll, and he shall wash them off into the water of bitterness. Then he shall make the woman drink the water of bitterness that brings a curse, so that the water which brings a curse will go into her and cause bitterness." Luke even picked up on Numbers 5:1-4 when he wrote about the leper, the hemorrhaging woman, and the dead little girl. Whereas every Old Testament member of the people of God would have told Jesus, "Don't touch this person, Jesus. It will make you unclean," instead, we are told by Luke that when Jesus touched the leper, He didn't become unclean; instead, the leper became clean (Luke 5:12-16).

A few chapters later, in Luke 8:40-56, Jesus was on His way to the house of a leader who would soon lose a child, and a woman who was hemorrhaging touched Him. Every Hebrew person there was thinking, *Oh no, she's unclean.* Yet something extraordinary happened, Luke recorded that Jesus didn't become unclean; rather, the woman became clean. A few moments later, Jesus came into the presence of a dead child and said, "Child, arise!" (verse 54). Even though Jesus had been in the proximity of a dead body, He was not made unclean. Rather, He restored life to this girl. We are told by Luke that this Lord Jesus is absolutely extraordinary; He makes the unclean clean.

Just after the apostle Paul referenced Numbers 5 in 1 Corinthians 11, he wrote, "In the same way He took the cup also after supper, saying, 'This cup is the new covenant in My blood; do this, as often as you drink it, in remembrance of Me'" (1 Corinthians 11:25). Then Paul said, "A man must examine himself, and in so doing he is to eat of the bread and drink of the cup. For he who eats and drinks, eats and drinks judgment to himself if he does not judge the body rightly" (1 Corinthians 11:28-29). Jesus knew what was in that cup, and the only One who could drink it was Him, or those who are in Him by the Spirit, by grace, through faith. For anyone else to drink that cup meant that they would come under its just condemnation. But He drank the cup, and He drank it to the dregs.

Jesus wrestled in the Garden of Gethsemane over this: "My Father, if it is possible, let this cup pass from Me" (Matthew 26:39). He spoke this way because He knew what was in the cup. Just as the priests wrote the words of this curse, scraped them into the water, and handed the water to the woman, do you see what your Savior was doing for you on the cross? He was drinking your cup. Like those good Hebrews who watched Him come near to touch the leper, the hemorrhaging woman, and the dead child, we're all saying, "Lord God, don't drink that cup of mine. Don't

infect Yourself with my judgment, my condemnation. My sins are written on that sheet. Don't take that into Your body."

But He still drinks the cup, and He drinks to the dregs for those from
every tribe, tongue, people, and nation, men and women, and boys and
girls, all who trust in Him. By the taking of that cup, and by the shedding
of His blood, He made you clean. Hallelujah, what a Savior! Lead your
people to find their purity in Christ alone by being clothed in His righteousness. And lead them to live out practically what they are positionally,
because impurity affects the entire camp.

PRAYER

Our Lord and our God, we believe that Your Word is
inspired, but we doubt it at times. We come to passages
like this, and we think that the light of the gospel cannot burst forth from them. Oh, how we love it when You
prove us wrong. We thank You for the glory of this passage, for the way that it points to the requirement of living out the Christian life, and most of all, how it points
to our Savior. He took the cup of judgment and curs-
ing in our place that we might become the righteousness
of God in Him. No one can pluck us out of His hands.
Guide us, indeed, O Thou, our great Jehovah. In Jesus'
name, Amen.

HALLOWED BE YOUR NAME: THE LEADER ON HIS KNEES

"Everyone who asks, receives; and he who seeks, finds;
and to him who knocks, it will be opened."

LUKE 11:10

3

HALLOWED BE YOUR NAME: THE LEADER ON HIS KNEES

Tom Pennington
Shepherds' Conference 2013

Luke 11:1-13

Nothing comes more naturally to us than breathing. From the doctor's first slap, it's involuntary. As you read this you are breathing somewhere between 12 and 15 times a minute, and today you will breathe 20,000 times. We can vary the rate of our breathing. We can even hold our breath for a short time, but it is impossible to voluntarily stop breathing entirely. If we don't inhale, carbon dioxide builds up in our blood and we experience what scientists refer to as "overwhelming air hunger."

This reflex is essential to human life. Without breathing, the body's oxygen level drops dangerously low in a short period of time. Within three to six minutes the brain is irreversibly damaged, and minutes later, death follows. You can live for weeks without food. You can live for days without water. But you can live for only a few minutes without oxygen.

Breathing is so crucial to living that breath is a metaphor for life itself. That's why the English Puritan Thomas Watson's statement is so arresting and compelling: "Prayer is the soul's breathing."[1] What breathing is to the body, praying is to the soul. We absolutely cannot survive without it. John

Calvin referred to prayer as the soul of faith. Just as the body dies when the soul leaves; even so, faith itself dies when prayer is gone.

Remarkably, in spite of the importance of prayer and our understanding of it, we pray very little. It's like exercise—we all know it's important, but for many of us, the greatest exertion each day is forcing the ice cream scoop into a frozen half-gallon container of ice cream.

A Shocking Census

Nearly 30 years ago, 17,000 Christians attended a conference sponsored by a major denomination. While they were there, they completed a survey about their spiritual habits and activities. It remains, as far as I know, the largest survey of its kind. Some 17,000 evangelical Christians were asked questions, including a question about how much time they spent in prayer on a daily basis. They reported that they prayed, on average, less than 5 minutes a day. At the same conference there were 2000 pastors and their wives, and they were asked the same question. On average, 2000 evangelical pastors and their wives reported that they prayed less than 7 minutes a day.[2]

It appears that prayer has in fact become the pastor's most neglected duty. Sadly, it's unlikely that those numbers have changed much in the ensuing years. In fact, I think in today's man-centered, shallow Christian culture, the situation is probably far worse. What makes those statistics so tragic is that Scripture tells us that the one true and living God actually listens to the prayers of His people. Psalm 34:17 says, "The righteous cry, and the LORD hears." Because of that spiritual reality, the hearts of the righteous have always beat with a passion for speaking to God.

The Blessing of Prayer

Before the fall, Adam and Eve walked and talked with the second member of the Trinity in the Garden. The first reference to prayer, as we know it, comes in Genesis chapter 4. We read that in the godly line of Seth, "men began to call upon the name of the LORD" (verse 25). From that point onward, prayer permeates the pages of the Old Testament. In the New Testament, prayer remains foundational to man's relationship to God. A devotion to prayer was the consistent pattern of the early church.

According to Acts 2:42, believers "were continually devoting themselves to the apostles' teaching and to fellowship, to the breaking of bread and to prayer."

Prayer was also the great priority of the apostle Paul. You're familiar with the many times he referred to his prayers. First Thessalonians 3:10: "We night and day keep praying most earnestly." Second Timothy 1:3: "I constantly remember you in my prayers night and day."

Nothing is more foundational to the health of our own Christian faith than prayer.

Throughout church history, godly men have joined the chorus, emphasizing the importance of prayer. Augustine wrote, "Prayer is the protection of holy souls...the preserver of spiritual health[3]...the column of all virtues, a ladder to God...[and] the foundation of faith."[4] Martin Luther said, "As it is the business of tailors to make clothes, and of cobblers to mend shoes, so it is the business of Christians to pray."[5] In his *Institutes*, John Calvin called prayer "the chief exercise of faith by which we daily receive God's benefits."[6]

Reasons We Don't Pray

Nothing is more foundational to the health of our own Christian faith than prayer. We all say we believe that and we affirm it. So the question is, Why don't we pray? What are the reasons we give for not praying? There really is only one reason that we typically offer, and it's that we don't have time. "I would like to pray more, but I'm just too busy" is the common excuse. But we must strip away that excuse for a moment and honestly remind ourselves that this is not the reason we don't pray. Busyness is just an excuse, a feeble attempt to justify our lack of obedience to the clear will of God. So what are the real reasons that we don't pray? Let me give you a few to consider.

One reason we don't pray is a lack of humility. We are by nature, as fallen sinners, fiercely independent. But independence is not a reflection of, nor is it the path to, spiritual maturity. Instead, spiritual maturity is marked by believing what our Lord taught us in John 15—that apart from Him we can do nothing. In 1 Peter 5, Peter called on us to humble ourselves under the mighty hand of God, to accept His providence in our lives (verses 6-7). That humility is expressed by casting all of our care upon Him, because He cares for us. When we are truly humbled before God, we will recognize our need of Him and we will pray. In fact, the clearest measure of our pride is our neglect to pray.

A second reason we don't pray is a lack of faith. Often we don't pray because, frankly, we haven't seen results when we have prayed. Past results, however, don't justify our lack of future efforts. This is a greater problem than we are willing to admit. Though we would never say prayer doesn't work, if we really believed that there would be clear, visible, verifiable results within five minutes of praying, then we would become prayer warriors. It often comes down to our doubting whether anything will happen when we pray. This frame of mind means nothing will happen, because, as James wrote, "Ask in faith without any doubting, for the one who doubts is like the surf of the sea, driven and tossed by the wind. For that man ought not to expect that he will receive anything from the Lord" (James 1:6-7).

A third reason we don't pray is a lack of obedience. We are commanded to pray. Romans 12:12: Be "devoted to prayer." Colossians 4:2: "Devote yourselves to prayer." First Thessalonians 5:17: "Pray without ceasing." Prayer is to be the constant daily pattern of our lives. So let's be honest with ourselves and with the Scriptures, and acknowledge that if we are not personally devoted to prayer, it is sin. We must obey our Lord and we must devote ourselves to prayer.

Growing in Prayer

The key question that arises is, How can we grow in our understanding and practice of this discipline? Nowhere do we learn more about how to pray than in what is traditionally called the Lord's Prayer. Two versions of the Lord's Prayer have been preserved for us through divine inspiration.

One is in Matthew 6:9-13, and the other in Luke 11:1-4. Now, these are not parallel passages. In harmonizing the Gospels, we discover that Jesus probably preached the Sermon on the Mount—recorded in Matthew 6— in the summer of AD 29, or the summer before His crucifixion if you hold to a different date of His death. A few months later, probably in the fall of that same year, Jesus taught Luke 11. This prayer, then, is one that Jesus repeated on at least two occasions, and He probably used it a number of other times throughout His ministry as a pattern for His disciples' prayers.

Luke's version of the Lord's Prayer is extremely insightful for us because of the circumstances in Luke 11:1-13. In verse 1, a disciple requests instruction on prayer, and that is followed in verses 2 through 4 by the Lord's Prayer. Our Lord gives us a pattern, then, for prayer. Verses 5 through 8 record the parable of the reluctant friend, a parable about God's eagerness to hear our prayers. In verses 9 through 10, our Lord gives us direct affirmation that God hears and answers prayer: "Ask, and it will be given to you; seek, and you will find; knock, and it will be opened to you. For everyone who asks, receives; and he who seeks, finds; and to him who knocks, it will be opened." In verses 11-13, Jesus ends this lesson on prayer by giving us an illustration from family life, which shows that God is even more responsive to the requests of His children than human fathers.

Notice the first four verses of Luke 11:

> It happened that while Jesus was praying in a certain place, after He had finished, one of His disciples said to Him, "Lord, teach us to pray just as John also taught his disciples." And He said to them, "When you pray, say: 'Father, hallowed be Your name. Your kingdom come. Give us each day our daily bread. And forgive us our sins, for we ourselves also forgive everyone who is indebted to us. And lead us not into temptation.'"

I want to focus primarily on verse 1 because it turns the spotlight onto Jesus' personal example of prayer. And it shows the impact that Jesus' example of prayer had on the disciples, and the impact it should have on us. By observing Jesus' example, we learn three crucial lessons about our own prayer life.

Prayer Requires Commitment

The first lesson is that prayer is a spiritual priority that requires great commitment. In verse 1 we read, "It happened that while Jesus was praying in a certain place..." The word Luke uses here for "praying" is the Greek word we expect. It's part of the family of words that the New Testament uses most frequently for prayer. In secular Greek, this word simply meant to speak to a deity. In Scripture, it is used of man's approach to God. It is, as Calvin defined prayer, "conversation with God."[7]

Here, our Lord speaks to God. Nowhere do we witness firsthand the importance and priority of prayer more than in the life of our Lord. The writer of Hebrews wrote, "In the days of His flesh, He offered up both prayers and supplications with loud crying and tears to the One able to save Him from death, and He was heard because of His piety" (5:7). Now, it's tempting to think that Jesus spent time in prayer because He missed the communion that He had always enjoyed with the Father, but this doesn't pass the theological test. Jesus' divine nature didn't change when He took on humanity. Although His human nature was bound to a body and could be in only one place at any time, His divine nature continued to fill the universe. The communion that the Son had enjoyed with the Father from all eternity continued throughout His earthly life, except for during those dark hours on the cross. This is foundational to our grasping the priority of prayer—Jesus' prayer life was a reflection of His human nature, not of His divine nature. It was as the perfect man living the life you and I should live that He prayed.

And He prayed often. In fact, nine times in this Gospel, Luke tells us about Jesus praying. We are told Jesus began his public ministry with prayer: "Now when all the people were baptized, Jesus was also baptized, and while He was praying, heaven was opened, and the Holy Spirit descended upon Him in bodily form like a dove, and a voice came out of heaven, 'You are My beloved Son, in You I am well-pleased'" (Luke 3:21-22). Jesus' public ministry, initiated at His baptism, began with prayer.

Luke wrote that this was Jesus' regular practice. For example Luke 5:16 says, "Jesus Himself would often slip away to the wilderness and pray." Literally, the text says, "He was withdrawing and was praying." Luke intended to stress for us the fact that this was a consistent pattern of Jesus'

life. We also learn that Jesus prayed all night before making a strategic decision. For example, He prayed before He chose the Twelve: "It was at this
time that He went off to the mountain to pray, and He spent the whole
night in prayer to God. And when day came, He called His disciples to
Him and chose twelve of them" (Luke 6:12-13). The choice of the Twelve
came out of a night of prayer.

According to Luke, it was while Jesus was praying that He was transfigured before the disciples. Luke 9:28-29 says, "Some eight days after
these sayings, He took along Peter and John and James, and went up on
the mountain to pray. And while He was praying, the appearance of His
face became different, and His clothing became white and gleaming." The
Father chose to reveal His glory while Jesus was praying. In Luke 22:39 we
find Jesus in Gethsemane praying, "And He came out"—that is, out of the
upper room—"and proceeded as was His custom to the Mount of Olives;
and the disciples also followed Him…" "And He withdrew from them
about a stone's throw, and He knelt down and began to pray" (22:41). He
even died praying: "Jesus, crying out with a loud voice, said, 'Father, into
Your hands I commit My Spirit.' Having said this, He breathed His last"
(23:46). Jesus' last words were a prayer of trust.

Now Mark's Gospel gives us additional insight. Mark makes it clear
that Jesus' typical day was filled with prayer. In Mark 1:35 we discover
that Jesus prayed early in the morning. This was His practice: "In the early
morning, while it was still dark, Jesus got up, left the house, and went away
to a secluded place, and was praying there." What makes this truly remarkable is that it happened on Sunday, after a very busy Sabbath. Notice in
verses 21-22 that Jesus had begun His day by teaching in the synagogue in
Capernaum. While He was there, He cast a demon out of a man (verses
23-28). He returned to Peter's home and there healed Peter's mother-in-
law (verses 29-31). All of this occurred before lunch, but the day was not
over for Jesus. In fact, after dark, when the Sabbath was over, the entire
city showed up outside of Peter's home (verse 33). This passage emphasizes
Jesus' personal interest in individuals; one by one He healed them and cast
out demons. Undoubtedly, that went on late into the night.

Early the next morning, Sunday, after that long day and night of ministry, Jesus got up to pray while it was still dark. So much for the excuse that

we don't have time. Jesus "went away to a secluded place"—literally to a wilderness (verse 35). He strategically slipped out of Peter's house, quietly left the city of Capernaum, and found a quiet, secluded place in order to have an extended time of prayer.

Not only did Jesus pray in the morning, He also prayed in the evening after a long day's work. We read in Mark 6:45-48,

> Immediately Jesus made His disciples get into the boat and go ahead of Him to the other side to Bethsaida, while He Himself was sending the crowd away. After bidding them farewell, He left for the mountain to pray. When it was evening, the boat was in the middle of the sea, and He was alone on the land. Seeing them straining at the oars, for the wind was against them, at about the fourth watch of the night He came to them, walking on the sea.

Now again what makes this remarkable is what had transpired earlier that day. Jesus' time of prayer came at the end of a long day, during which a crowd of more than 15,000 people had tracked Him down. Jesus' compassion led Him to heal the sick and, according to Mark 6:34, He taught them many things. Late that afternoon, on the same day, He had miraculously fed this crowd of 5000 men, which probably means more than 15,000 people altogether. It was after a day of intense ministry that Jesus spent time in prayer.

Jesus' example demonstrates that next to the Word of God, prayer was His greatest duty.

He also made it clear that He expects us, as His disciples, to pray as well. In Luke 11:2 our Lord said, "When you pray." In Matthew 6:5-7, He used that same phrase three separate times—"When you pray…when you pray…when you are praying." The first time He used a plural pronoun. It's as if He were saying, "When you—that is, *all* of My disciples—pray, and I'm assuming and expecting that you will."

But He went beyond expecting that we would pray— throughout the New Testament, He commanded us to pray. Read Ephesians 6:18: "With all prayer and petition pray at all times in the Spirit, and with this in view, be on the alert with all perseverance and petition for all the saints." In

Colossians 4:2 we are told, "Devote yourselves to prayer." The Christian life is not merely about the indicatives of the gospel, but as a result of our justification, there are also imperatives we are to obey. Praying is one of those spiritual imperatives, a command from our Lord Himself.

The priorities of Jesus and the priorities of His apostles must be our priorities as well.

No matter how busy we are, there is absolutely no excuse not to pray. The two compelling priorities in Jesus' ministry were the Word of God and prayer. The apostles, like us, could be pretty dense, but they eventually got this. In Acts 6:4, you read that the apostles in the Jerusalem church were devoting themselves to prayer and the ministry of the Word. The priorities of Jesus and the priorities of His apostles must be our priorities as well.

Prayer Is Necessary for Effective Ministry

Prayer is essential for all Christians, but it is even more vital for us who are the leaders of His church, because it is the foundation of all ministry. You see this in the apostle Paul, specifically his prayers, because they were the foundation of the effective ministry that he enjoyed. Paul's ministry existed because God responded to his prayers.

We also see this in the examples of other Christian leaders in the church, specifically the example of Epaphras, who was a leader in the church in Colossae. When Paul addressed the Colossian church, he wrote, "Epaphras, who is one of your number, a bondslave of Jesus Christ, sends you his greetings, always laboring earnestly for you in his prayers, that you may stand perfect and fully assured in all the will of God" (4:12). John Owen, the great English Puritan, said, "He that is more frequent in his pulpit to his people than he is in his closet for his people is but a sorry watchman."[8] Jonathan Edwards wrote of David Brainerd, "His history shows us the right way to success in the work of the ministry…How did he labor always fervently…in prayers day and night, wrestling with God in secret…until

Christ [was] formed in the hearts of the people to whom he was sent!"[9] Prayer is a spiritual imperative.

Prayer Is Necessary for Effective Preaching

Prayer is also essential to effective preaching. The apostle Paul understood this and asked the Ephesians, "Pray on my behalf, that utterance may be given to me in the opening of my mouth, to make known with boldness the mystery of the gospel" (Ephesians 6:19). Augustine wrote, "A preacher must labor to be heard with understanding, with willingness, and with obedience. Let him not doubt that he will affect this with fervent prayers more than with all the power of his oratory."[10] Richard Baxter wrote, "Prayer must carry on our work as well as our preaching. For he that does not pray for his people will not preach powerfully to his people."[11]

Prayer Is Necessary for the Battle with Temptation

It is also through prayer that we win the personal battle with temptation and sin. In Luke 22:39-46, our Lord connected prayer with the power to overcome temptation. "Watch and pray that you do not enter into temptation." Commenting on the final petition in the Lord's Prayer, John Calvin wrote, "We conclude from this petition that we have no strength for living a godly life except so far as we obtain it from God. Whoever implores the assistance of God to overcome temptations acknowledges that unless God deliver him he will be constantly falling."[12] J.C. Ryle wrote, "What is the reason that some believers are so much brighter and holier than others? I believe the difference, in nineteen cases out of twenty, arises from different habits about private prayer. I believe that those who are not eminently holy pray *little*, and those who are eminently holy pray *much*."[13] It sounds simplistic to say that our spiritual struggles stem from the neglect of either Scripture or prayer. But when people come into the pastor's office seeking counsel, nine times out of ten they have been inconsistent either in private prayer, in the Word, or both. If you are losing in your struggle with a sin habit, it is probably because you are neglecting one or both of the basic means through which God extends His grace to us, and that is through His Word and prayer. John Owen, in his classic work on sin and temptation, makes this point:

A man finds any lust…[that] is powerful, strong, tumultuating, leads captive, vexes, disquiets, takes away peace; he is not able to bear it; wherefore, he sets himself against it, prays against it, groans under it, sighs to be delivered: but in the meantime, perhaps, in other duties—constant communion with God— in reading, prayer, and meditation—he is loose and negligent. Let not that man think that ever he shall arrive to the mortification of the lust he is perplexed with…Do you think he will ease you of that which perplexes you, so that you may be at liberty to that which no less grieves Him? No. God says, "Here is one, if he could be rid of this lust I should never hear of him more; let him wrestle with this, or he is lost." Let not any man think to do his own work that will not do God's. God's work consists in universal obedience; to be freed of the present perplexity is their own only…The rage and predominance of a particular lust is commonly the fruit and issue of a careless, negligent course in general.[14]

As the disciples watched Jesus' life, they saw Him praying. It's clear from Luke 11:1 that they came to the conclusion that prayer was a spiritual priority in His life, and therefore must be in their own lives as well. Without prayer, spiritual growth is impossible, and ministry will be totally ineffective.

Lessons About Prayer
Prayer Requires Deliberate Time

The first lesson we learn from Jesus' example is that prayer is a spiritual priority that requires great commitment. If that is true, why do we so frequently neglect this duty? I think we can see why in the second lesson that we learn from Luke 11:1—prayer is an intentional practice that requires deliberate time.

Notice again verse 1: "It happened that while Jesus was praying in a certain place, after He had finished…" The clear implication of this statement is that the disciples saw Jesus praying, they saw the priority in His life, and they had to wait until He finished praying. In other words, Jesus devoted time to prayer. In other places, the Gospel writers tell us that our

Lord spent considerable time in prayer. He often withdrew to a lonely place to pray, and that would have been pointless if He intended to spend only a short time in prayer. We are told that on at least two occasions, Jesus prayed all night.

We can gain further insight into our Lord's prayer life by looking at what happened during the Passion Week. The Thursday night before His crucifixion, Jesus and His disciples assembled in the upper room to celebrate the Passover. In Luke 22, we learn that Jesus had prayed for Peter, that his faith not fail. Of course, as they gathered to celebrate the traditional Passover celebration, Jesus, as the host, would have offered a number of prayers. In addition to that, He inaugurated the Lord's Table and gave thanks for both the bread and the cup. When the supper was over, Jesus prayed what is the longest recorded prayer from Him in Scripture—it appears in John 17 and is often called His high-priestly prayer.

Afterward, Jesus and the disciples left the upper room and went to Gethsemane, where again Jesus prayed—three times. Jesus prayed long enough that Peter, James, and John fell asleep. It's likely that Jesus prayed at least an hour and maybe as long as two hours. Our Lord offered all of those prayers in just one evening between sunset and midnight. Clearly, He devoted deliberate and intentional time to praying. Yet we are tempted to use Paul's words, "Pray without ceasing" (1 Thessalonians 5:17) to justify our lack of time spent in prayer. This is how we salve our consciences. It's true that our lives are to be lived in a spirit of prayer, but the same apostle who wrote "Pray without ceasing" also wrote "Devote yourselves to prayer" (Colossians 4:2). Prayer requires deliberate and intentional time.

But why is prayer not the habitual practice of our lives? At a practical level, one reason is that we simply don't have undistracted time. The average person is interrupted by his smartphone, phone calls, text messages, and Facebook updates every three minutes. According to Nielsen Media Research, the average person in the US spends five hours a day watching videos, and another hour using the Internet. If you're between the ages of 18 and 34, you spend almost three hours a day playing video games.[15] Although we should pray, we are constantly distracted by our electronic tools and toys. Turn off the television, turn off the game console, silence the smartphone, close the computer, and deliberately, intentionally get alone with God in prayer just as our Lord did.

A more subtle enemy to prayer is evident in Acts 6:2-4, where we read about the problem of feeding the widows in the church. The Twelve summoned the congregation of the disciples and said, "It is not desirable for us to neglect the word of God in order to serve tables. Therefore, brethren, select from among you seven men of good reputation, full of the Spirit and of wisdom, whom we may put in charge of this task. But we will devote ourselves to prayer and to the ministry of the word." Ministry itself and the legitimate needs of people threatened to destroy the apostles' devotion to the Word of God and to prayer. The same is true for us. The good is often the enemy of the best, and the busyness of ministry can destroy our devotion to the Word of God and to prayer. Like the apostles, we must not allow the busyness of ministry to eclipse prayer. Instead, find capable people who can come alongside you and free you for devotion to the Word of God and prayer.

Throughout Scripture we find others who intentionally set aside time each day for prayer. David, in Psalm 55:17, wrote, "Evening and morning and at noon, I will complain and murmur, and He will hear my voice." According to Daniel 6:10, even though Daniel knew about the decree prohibiting worship, he continued to kneel on his knees three times a day and pray and give thanks before his God as he had always done. In Acts 3:1, we read that Peter and John went up to the temple at the ninth hour, the hour of prayer. In Acts 10:9, we see that Peter went up on the housetop about the sixth hour, or noon, to pray. There was a daily, intentional pattern to these people's prayers.

Martin Luther's barber, Peter Beskendorf, once asked Luther about prayer. Luther wrote him a 40-page response. A portion of that response reads:

> A good clever barber must have his thoughts, mind and eyes concentrated upon the razor and the beard and not forget where he is in his stroke and shave. If he keeps talking or looking around or thinking of something else, he is likely to cut a man's mouth or nose—or even his throat. So anything that

is to be done well ought to occupy the whole man with all his faculties and members. As the saying goes: he who thinks of many things thinks of nothing and accomplishes no good. How much more must prayer possess the heart exclusively and completely if it is to be a good prayer?...It is a good thing to let prayer be the first business in the morning and the last in the evening. Guard yourself against such false and deceitful thoughts that keep whispering: Wait a little while. In an hour or so I will pray, I must first finish this or that. Thinking such thoughts we get away from prayer into other things that will hold us and involve us till the prayer of that day comes to naught.[16]

The main difference between those who pray and those who don't is that those who pray *plan* to pray. Calvin included an entire section in the *Institutes* entitled "Prayer At Regular Times," in which he suggested a daily pattern of prayer: When you first get up, when you start your work, before meals, and at the end of the day.[17] We've learned from the life of our Lord that prayer was an intentional practice for which He deliberately set aside time. If it was so important for Him to make time to pray during a ministry of only three-and-a-half years, how much more important is it for us! His ministry was far more demanding than ours, and yet He made time to pray. May we never insult our Lord again by saying the reason we don't pray is because we don't have enough time. Jesus' example teaches us that prayer is a spiritual priority that requires great commitment, and that prayer is an intentional practice that requires we deliberately set aside time for it.

Prayer Requires Careful Instruction

The third lesson we learn from Luke 11:1 is that prayer is a practical skill that requires careful instruction. "It happened that while Jesus was praying in a certain place, after He had finished, one of His disciples said to Him, 'Lord, teach us to pray just as John also taught his disciples.'" One of the Twelve—we aren't told here which one—makes this specific request: "Lord teach us to pray." "Teach" here is translated from a common Greek verb that refers to oral instruction. The disciples already had a basic understanding of prayer because they had read the Old Testament and the examples of prayer that appear there. They had grown up in Jewish homes in which they had heard praying, and they themselves had prayed. By the time this incident occurs in Luke 11, they had lived with Jesus Christ day and night for more than a year. They had undoubtedly heard Him pray many times before. And just a few months earlier—in the summer of that year—Jesus had taught them how to pray when He taught the Sermon on the Mount. But they still had not mastered the skill.

In one sense, praying is just the natural cry of a child to his Father, but mature praying doesn't come naturally. It is a skill that must be taught and learned. The disciples knew that their prayers still needed help, and they weren't the only ones to acknowledge their inadequacy in this area. They said, "Teach us to pray just as John [the Baptist] also taught his disciples." We have no record of John's prayers or of his teaching on prayer, but clearly this was an essential part of his ministry. In fact, in Luke 5:33, the Pharisees said to Jesus, "The disciples of John often fast and offer prayers." John's disciples needed to be taught how to pray, just as the apostles requested Jesus to teach them how to pray.

This point should be very comforting. We aren't the only ones who need help with prayer. We get in line behind the disciples of John and behind the apostles when it comes to learning how to pray. We also see here that prayer is a skill we can acquire with the right instruction. Of course, the best One to teach us how to pray is Jesus Himself. The amazing truth is that, by the grace of God, we have an inspired record of how our Lord taught His disciples to pray. The answer to the request in verse 1 is found in verse 2: "He said to them, 'When you pray, say...'" and of course what follows is the Lord's Prayer. Jesus gave the most comprehensive version of this prayer a few months earlier, when He preached the Sermon on the Mount.

In Matthew 6:9, Jesus began, "Pray, then, in this way." Jesus here provided us with a model and a pattern to fashion all our prayers after. Just as the Ten Commandments condensed God's law into ten Hebrew words that even a child could memorize, this prayer condenses everything that should be a part of our prayers into a small package that even a child can learn. Hugh Latimer, the English Reformer and martyr, described it this way: "This prayer is the sum and abridgment of all other prayers. All other prayers are contained in this prayer."[18]

In this remarkable prayer, our Lord gave us a model that our prayer should follow. It is important for us to make a couple observations about this prayer that ought to encourage us to study our Lord's instruction more carefully.

The Elements of Prayer

There are three elements of this prayer: a preface, six petitions, and a conclusion. The preface, "Our Father who is in heaven," teaches us the attitude that we should have as we come before God in prayer. "Our" is a plural pronoun. Prayer is not an individualistic, self-absorbed practice. Rather, we are to pray as a member of a family. The word "Father" reminds us that we are to pray as a child to his father. We've been adopted, and therefore we're talking to our Father. The balance comes in the expression "who is in heaven." This means that we are not only to come to Him as to our Father, but also as a subject to a King.

The six petitions that follow identify six categories of prayer. They outline the kinds of requests that should come from our lips and our hearts. We are to pray for *the glory of God*—"hallowed be Your name." That is, may His name and everything connected with Him be set apart and treated as holy. We are to pray for the *kingdom of God*—"Your kingdom come." We should pray for the advancement of God's spiritual kingdom in people's hearts and for the coming of the literal kingdom when our Lord returns and establishes it. Third, we are to pray for *the will of God*—"Your will be done on earth as it is in heaven." Fourth, we are to pray for *the needs of this life*—"Give us this day our daily bread." Fifth, we are to pray for *the confession of sin*—"Forgive us our debts as we have forgiven our debtors." And sixth, we are to pray for *the pursuit of holiness*—"Do not lead us into temptation, but deliver us from evil."

Notice the proportion of these requests: half are about God, and half are about us and our needs. Notice the balance in this model prayer—Jesus divided the requests that we should be making of God into six categories, and yet most of our prayers fall into only two of them: the needs of this life, and the confession of sin. That means our prayers are significantly out of balance. Also, observe the order of the requests, which is obviously by design and tells us volumes about the focus of our prayers. The first three are all about God. Our needs come only in the second half of this prayer. That means our prayers must begin with and be preoccupied with God, His glory, His kingdom, and His will. Only then are we ready to ask for the things that we need.

What is remarkable about this prayer is that Jesus taught us to pray the same way He prayed. Jesus often began His prayers by addressing God as His Father and acknowledging that He is in heaven. Luke 10:21: "I praise you, Oh, Father, Lord of heaven and earth." He was always concerned in prayer that His Father's name be hallowed: "Father, glorify Your name" (John 12:28). We read in John 17:1, "Lifting up His eyes to heaven, He said, 'Father, the hour has come; glorify Your Son, that the Son may glorify You.'"

Jesus constantly prayed that God's kingdom would advance. In John 11:41-42 He said, "Father, I thank You that You have heard Me. I knew that You always hear Me; but because of the people standing around I said it, so that they may believe that You sent me." Jesus' concern was that God's will be done on earth. In the Garden of Gethsemane He prayed, "Father, if You are willing, remove this cup from Me; yet not My will, but Yours be done" (Luke 22:42). He prayed regarding the needs of this life, including the need for daily bread. We always find Jesus praying before meals and praying before He miraculously produced food for the crowds.

Although Jesus never asked forgiveness for His own sins—because He had none—He did pray for the forgiveness of others. In Luke 23:34 He asked, "Father, forgive them." He also prayed for the spiritual protection and growth of others—in Luke 22:32 He told Peter that though Satan wanted to sift him like wheat, "I have prayed for you, that your faith may not fail." In John 17:17, Jesus prayed for His apostles and for us when He said, "Sanctify them in the truth; Your word is truth." When you pray in the same categories that appear in the Lord's Prayer, you join your prayer with the Lord Himself. Right now, our great High Priest continues to offer these same petitions with us and for us. He ever lives to make intercession for us.

Our Lord has shown us the priority of prayer in our lives and ministries by His own personal example. He has shown us the practice of prayer by the time He deliberately and intentionally invested in it. And He has taught us the skill of prayer by His careful instruction. He has given us everything that we need. Now we need to simply ask for the grace to determine, as His apostles did, that we will devote ourselves to the ministry of the Word and to prayer.

PRAYER

Father, forgive us for excusing our lack of obedience. Forgive us for our lack of faith. Forgive us for sinning against You and our people by not praying as we should, by not being devoted as our Lord was to prayer. We pray that today, You would give us a renewed commitment to devote ourselves daily to intentional, deliberate prayer. We pray in Jesus' name, Amen.

A Leader Who Suffers Well

"I rejoice in my sufferings for your sake."

Colossians 1:24

4

A Leader Who Suffers Well

John Piper

Shepherds' Conference 2001

Colossians 1:24

Opening Prayer

Father, I ask that the effect of our efforts would be radical obedience. I also pray for a readiness to suffer for the cause of Christ, and a readiness to take risks that would look foolish and be foolish where there is no resurrection from the dead. I pray that we would be freed from the American vise grip of ease, comfort, security, and safety. I pray that You will keep me faithful to Your Word now, balanced in its proportions, protected from the devil, and filled with Your Spirit, leaving out anything unhelpful and including all that should be mentioned for the strengthening of God's people. In Jesus' name, Amen.

Tribulation and Joy

We read in 1 Thessalonians 1:6, "You also became imitators of us and of the Lord." In this text there are two people who are models of something, namely Jesus and Paul. Here is what they are models of: "having received the word in much tribulation with joy of the Holy Spirit." Jesus was a man who received the Word of God in tribulation, but was sustained by joy. We read in Hebrews, "For the joy [that was] set before Him [He] endured the cross" (Hebrews 12:2). Paul was a man who received the Word of God and was told in receiving of it, "I will show Him how much He must suffer for My name's sake" (Acts 9:16). Yet the apostle said over and over again that he rejoiced in tribulation. We are called to be imitators of Jesus and Paul. We are called to receive the Word in much tribulation, but with joy.

Paul lived a life of suffering. The question is: What was the function of suffering in the apostle's life? Or what is the function of the suffering in the pastor's life, the missionary's life, and the saint's life? Is it something that just happens to a pastor, and then that person can honor God because of the way he deals with it? Or is there a purpose for it in the church? Can a pastor suffer for his church? Can he suffer for his mission field?

Is suffering just something that comes because the devil is a bad person and we then convert it into sanctifying influences through the power of the Holy Spirit? Or could it be that when God said to Paul, "I will show you how much you must suffer," that then there is a design and strategy in this suffering? I bring these questions and this topic up because leaders need to hear about suffering. Most pastors come from well-to-do churches, where very few people realize that they suffer by design.

Suffering as Strategy

Richard Wurmbrand was a Romanian pastor who suffered for 14 years in prison for the sake of the gospel. I learned from him by literally sitting at his feet, since he takes his shoes off and sits down when he speaks. It was about 15 years ago when I was with about 12 other pastors sitting low at Richard's feet, and it was then that he sowed into my heart the seed of embracing suffering as a strategy.

He asked questions like, "If you and the man next to you knew that both of you were about to have a child, one disabled, the other whole, which would you choose to have?" Even that question had a profound impact on me, and I've recently seen some ways it has influenced my flock. At Bethlehem Baptist, dozens of babies are adopted—from all over the United States and all over the world. Families are willing to endure suffering by adopting these little children from orphanages in Ukraine. The result is pain, and if God is merciful, glory. Some of these families have endured such pain that they've had to consider letting these kids go, and the pain of that is incredible. These families have put themselves in life-threatening situations because of their choice to love and ultimately because of their choice to suffer.

Richard Wurmbrand has also impacted me through a story that he told. It was a story about a Cistercian monk, which is an order in the Catholic Church that is always quiet. A radio interviewer in Italy asked this abbot of the Cistercian monastery, "What if you were to realize at the end of your life that atheism is true, and that there is no God?" And the abbot replied, "Holiness, silence, and sacrifice are beautiful in themselves. Even without the promise of a reward, I still will have used my life well." Paul, however, would have given the exact opposite answer, because he did give the exact opposite answer in 1 Corinthians 15:19. Paul wrote, "If we have hoped in Christ in this life only, we are of all men most to be pitied." There's not a text in the last ten years of my life that has caused me more difficulty than this passage, brought me to my face, called my ministry into question, and threatened to change my future more than this text.

This passage says that if there is no resurrection from the dead, then the choices I am making and the life I am living are absolutely absurd. This kind of thinking is shocking in America because almost nobody sells Christianity this way. People sell Christianity as love, joy, peace, patience, kindness, better marriage, and more obedient kids. Even a God who perhaps prospers your business. Consequently, if Christianity is a delusion, then it does not make a difference as long as you've lived a good life.

However, Paul had the opposite view. We are of all men most to be laughed at, pitied, regarded as foolish and absurd if we are not raised from the dead after this hellish life. Paul did explain in the same chapter the alternative option if there is no resurrection from the dead. He wrote, "Let us eat and drink" (15:32). Now, he didn't mean by that we should all become drunkards and gluttons if there's no resurrection. To be a glutton and be overweight means having a heart attack when you're 36. Or to be a drunkard entails a difficult life. Nobody looks at those modes of life and says, "There's the life." What Paul meant is, "Just be normal." Eat, drink, be normal, avoid any excessive risks, keep the security high, and enjoy reasonable comforts. That is how one is to live if there's no resurrection from the dead. Normal, simple, ordinary, cultural Christianity if there is no resurrection.

Paul further explained how the truth of the resurrection impacted his life in 1 Corinthians 15:29-31: "If the dead are not raised…why are we also in danger every hour?" I read that on the plane today and thought to myself, "Good night." If I'm in peril even one hour, I will try to fix it. I naturally do not want to be in peril, but Paul chose it. For Paul, it wasn't just one hour, it was every day, all day. Danger on the seas, danger on the roads, danger in the city, danger from faulty brethren, and danger from the enemy. Paul did not have security, and it seems like he was always in danger.

I've been in danger just a few times in my neighborhood when threats have come. As a result, it's tough to concentrate and do ministry. How are you going to prepare to talk to the Muslims tomorrow if the mob is outside tonight? Though in peril every hour, Paul went on to write, "I affirm, brethren, by the boasting in you which I have in Christ Jesus our Lord, I die daily" (15:31). Now that's foolish if there's no resurrection from the dead. If there's no assurance of resurrection from the dead, then you should get maximum life every day. This man thought this way, this man made these kinds of choices because he knew true joy. Paul's answer for suffering well is found in Colossians 1:24.

An Intimidating Text

In John MacArthur's office there is this brass statue of a man on his knees with his hands out. On the statue is written, "I will trust in the Lord." This statue of a man cringing face down before Almighty God is how I feel before these types of passages. As pastors, we are sometimes tempted to use the Bible in order to escape the Bible. We use expository preaching as the means for ministry to protect ourselves from passages that stretch us to minister in other ways. Don't get me wrong, I believe in expository preaching with all my heart, but God calls us to be more than just expositors.

Rejoice in Suffering

We read in Colossians 1:24, "Now I rejoice in my sufferings for your sake." We don't know what to do with a verse like this. Almost everyone in my church does the complete opposite—they grumble when they suffer; they ask God, "Why?" and they don't rejoice. What's wrong with the apostle Paul? Does he come from another planet? Yet the biblical pattern of life is so supernatural, so radical, and so different that very few pastors and laymen are living it.

We continue reading, "Now I rejoice in my sufferings for your sake, and in my flesh I do my share on behalf of His body, which is the church, in filling up what is lacking in Christ's afflictions." Paul labels his suffering as the "filling up what is lacking in Christ's afflictions." Suffering is designed to accomplish something called "filling up" what is lacking in Christ's afflictions. What does this mean? We all know what it does not mean. We know from Paul and Jesus that this verse does not mean that the apostle Paul improves upon the atoning work of the cross. When Jesus declared, "It is finished," He meant an infinitely valuable and perfect sacrifice has been made, and nobody can ever improve upon that sacrifice. What has been paid on the cross is paid in full, and no one can make any contribution to the payment that was made for the forgiveness of sins and the justification of lives before a holy God. Jesus alone has done this, and we find our security by resting in it.

So if that is what this verse does not mean, then what does it mean? What is lacking in the afflictions of Christ is not the perfection of the value of its atoning worth, but the personal presentation to those for whom He paid the price. Christ, by the Father's design, means for His atoning sufferings to be offered and presented to all those for whom He died, in every people group in the world; and this is to be done through suffering.

Joy is the only way you'll survive your mission in this world if you decide to suffer for Christ.

However, this suffering must be accompanied with joy, because without it one will never survive. For the joy that was set before Christ, He endured the cross. And for the joy that is set before you, you will endure the choices that you make, which make no sense if there's no resurrection from the dead. Joy is the only way you'll survive your mission in this world if you decide to suffer for Christ. The joy of the Lord will be your strength through choices that nobody understands.

A Parallel Example

Now, why do I think this passage means what I just said it means? Because of the parallel use of language in Philippians 2. I took the two key terms in this passage, "fill up" and "lacking," and searched where else these terms were paired. The clearest parallel example is found in Philippians 2, when Paul wrote about Epaphroditus. Epaphroditus was the individual who took the gifts from the Philippians to Rome, where Paul was. Paul responded to the Philippians with this letter and commended Epaphroditus because he risked his life almost to the point of death, according to Philippians 2:27. Epaphroditus made a choice that would have been pretty foolish to the world, but nonetheless, he made it. We read that he survived because "God had mercy on him" (verse 27). Therefore, Paul told the church to receive him with joy and to hold him and others like him in high regard.

In verse 30 we read that Epaphroditus "came close to death for the work of Christ, risking his life to complete what was deficient in your service to me." We see in this verse the two words found in Colossians 1:24, *lacking* and *fill up*. Here we have a very close parallel. The Philippians had a love gift for Paul; they were willing to sacrifice in order to serve a fellow brother in Christ. Yet this gift is incomplete until the Philippians get it to be where it was designed to be—in Rome. And Epaphroditus fills up what is lacking with the cost of almost his own life.

Marvin Vincent, who wrote a commentary on Philippians a little over 100 years ago, wrote on this passage, "The gift to Paul was a gift to the church as a body. It was a sacrificial offering of love. What was lacking was the church's presentation of this offering in person."[1]

Paul represented Epaphroditus as supplying what was lacking by his affectionate and zealous ministry. And that's my interpretation of Colossians 1:24—I think that's exactly what's going on in that verse. Jesus Christ has an affectionate sacrifice and offering for the world. He has designed that it not be telecast or radioed only, but embodied. Now, here's the question: If the design is to get the atoning, effective, powerful, gospel-feeling sufferings of Jesus into the lives of those for whom it was designed, by what means shall it happen? Paul made it very clear by what means in Colossians 1:24: "I rejoice in my sufferings for your sake...in filling up what is lacking."

The method for the "filling up" the "lack" of personal presentation is what happened to Paul's body when he preached:

> Five times I received from the Jews thirty-nine lashes. Three times I was beaten with rods, once I was stoned, three times I was shipwrecked, a night and a day I have spent in the deep. I have been on frequent journeys, in dangers from rivers, dangers from robbers, dangers from my countrymen, dangers from the Gentiles, dangers in the city, dangers in the wilderness, dangers on the sea, dangers among false brethren; I have been in labor and hardship, through many sleepless nights, in hunger and thirst, often without food, in cold and exposure (2 Corinthians 11:24-27).

Suffering is essential! Don't be a pastor if you don't believe that. God means for you to reach His people among all of the people groups of the world and in our neighborhoods with faithfulness in the midst of suffering. He means for those people to see Jesus, the real crucified Jesus, in your crucifixion. That's what Paul was writing in Colossians 1:24.

A Common Occurrence

I recently received a letter, and I'm going to use some false names here because I don't know if this person wants this out. The letter reads, "Two weeks ago, my brother, Joe, was shot as he sat in his hut in a northern Uganda village. Joe and his wife, Frances, are missionaries to the Muslim tribe Aringa in northern Uganda, which is three miles from Sudanese border. Frances and Joy, their five-month-old daughter, had just arrived in the States for a short visit since they'd been gone over a year. Joe remained in Africa. Two days after Frances's arrival, Joe and Martin were sitting together in the living area in the hut in the evening when they heard a strange sound outside. Joe suspected trouble. He jumped up, kicked the door shut just before the spray of bullets was released. The bullets exploded through the door, hit Joe in his shoulder and Martin in the lower arm."

The letter continues to explain that the assailants broke in, demanded money as they dragged the two men around, and these men cried out for Jesus to save them. What happened? The soldiers lowered their weapons and walked away. The men spent five hours without any medical aid and they still survived. That story had a happy ending, but we all know the stories that have the less "earthly" happy ending.

This is normal! Woe to the church that doesn't teach their young people that this is normal. Paul wrote, "I rejoice in my sufferings for your sake… in filling up what is lacking." Now, is this just apostolic? No, because Jesus declared, "For whoever wishes to save his life will lose it, but whoever loses his life for My sake and the gospel's will save it" (Mark 8:35).

The truth of suffering for the glory of God applies to everyone.

Beloved, the path of salvation is the path of losing one's life for the sake of the gospel. We also read in 2 Timothy 3:12, "Indeed, all who desire to live godly in Christ Jesus will be persecuted."

That truth of suffering for the glory of God applies to everyone. And the reason this truth finds so little echo in the American church is because we have so domesticated the word *godliness*—so much so that we scarcely can begin to comprehend what Paul meant by it. Godliness is limited to reading your Bible, going to church, and keeping the commandments. But that's not all there is to godliness because the Pharisees did all of those things. Godliness is being so ravished by God, so satisfied by God, so filled with God, so driven by Jesus that you live in a way that the only explanation for your life is the promise of God raising you from the dead. That's why I'm always praying, "Lord, get me and my wife ready for our next decision."

We will never be Christ's church until we choose to take risks that can only be explained by the resurrection from the dead. That's the only way that we'll be the church that we ought to be and finish the Great Commission.

Joy Is the Key to Suffering

The last word to investigate here is *joy.* "I rejoice in my sufferings." The Calvary road is a hard road filled with joy and Paul's joy seems to me to be absolutely boundless. He wrote to the Corinthians, "Sorrowful yet always rejoicing" (2 Corinthians 6:10). What is the key to this joy? We find it in Romans 5:2: "We exult in hope of the glory of God." Paul continued, "Not only this, but we also exult in our tribulations." I just read this morning an article by Marvin Olasky on the topic of proselytizing in the current issue of *World* magazine. He mentioned that Christianity has excellent examples of how to proselytize. But he also uses an illustration of bad ways to do it. He wrote that 100 years ago, in Turkey, Muslims lined up Armenian Christians and certain Muslim leaders would walk down the line and ask the question, "Do you worship Christ or Allah?" If the answer was "Christ," a sword was thrust to the abdomen. Now, how many people do you watch that happen to before you make up your mind as to what you will answer? Joy in Christ at that moment is not optional; it is the only hope of obedience. That's why Paul says here, "I rejoice in my sufferings."

Filling Up What Is Lacking

I want to conclude with an illustration from J. Oswald Sanders, a great statesman missionary. Sanders died a few years ago, and he was 89 when I heard him last. He gave an illustration which so perfectly embodies Colossians 1:24. Sanders talked about an Indian evangelist, a brand new believer who wanted to tell everybody about Jesus. He traveled the whole day and after a very difficult journey came to a village. He wondered whether he should wait until the morning to evangelize to this village. But then he decided to go into the village and preach the gospel before resting. The evangelist got the crowd around him, preached the gospel, and they scoffed at him. He quit because he was tired and discouraged, walked out of the village, and laid down underneath a tree to sleep.

A few hours later as the sun was going down, he woke up startled with the whole village around him. He saw one of the leaders of the village over him and thought, *Oh, they're going to hurt me or kill me.* The leader said, "We came out to see you and noticed the bloody feet that you have. We've decided that you must be a holy man and that you care about us because you came so far as to have feet like this. We would like to hear your message again."

Pastor, we rejoice in our sufferings, and in our flesh we fill up what is lacking in the afflictions of Jesus. One thing that is lacking in the afflictions of Jesus is a personal, embodied, bloody presentation of His cross to those for whom He died. We must be that presentation. I've preached this message multiple times because I feel burdened to call the church to get ready not for what may happen, but for what *should* happen if we're living Paul's life. You are being called through my mouth by God Almighty to make choices in your ministry, in your marriage, and in your parenting. If you are hovering right on the brink of a radical decision, I'm excited for you. I want to push you over the edge and reinforce what God is calling you to do, and that is to make choices in the service of love, not masochism—a service of suffering and sacrifice that can only be explained if Christ will raise you from the dead.

PRAYER

Father, I pray for pastors who teach these truths to their people. I pray that these leaders may build radical, out-of-sync, risk-taking, sacrificial, love-displaying, and Christ-exalting congregations. Congregations that can only be explained by the truth that Jesus has so satisfied their souls, that they can say, "Let goods and kindred go, this mortal life also; the body they may kill; God's truth abideth still; His kingdom is forever."[2] But Lord, You will never build these kinds of congregations if we don't embrace those risks of love. Show every person now the steps they are to take for the world to be stunned and give glory to our Father in heaven. In Christ's name I pray, Amen.

A Ministry of Integrity

"Knowing the fear of the Lord, we persuade men."

2 Corinthians 5:11

5

A Ministry of Integrity

John MacArthur

Shepherds' Conference 2010

2 Corinthians 5:11-15

I never think about the cross in vague or general terms. I always think about the death of Christ in a very personal way, mindful of the fact that Jesus bore in His own body my sins and credited His righteousness to my account. This truth lifts my worship to Him, and it reminds me that I am called to be a leader with integrity.

I recently spoke to a pastor who called me because he had put himself in a position of compromise. His actions were public and the people who were nearest and dearest to him were concerned about his behavior. I reminded him, along with any leader who reads this, that pastors are called to have integrity.

Levels of Integrity

First, integrity must be manifested in the pastor's family. You must make sure that the life you live so well matches the message that you preach to your children, wife, and the people close to you.

Second, the pastor is called to have integrity in the church. One of the downsides of spending nearly half a century in the same church is that there are no secrets. I don't have any secrets personally, nor does my family.

There is a great level of exposure in long-term ministry. The upside is if by the grace, goodness, and kindness of God a pastor can survive with his integrity intact, there is a joy and a level of trust that exists in the church family that is difficult to describe.

Third, a pastor must have integrity with the people beyond his own church who are influenced by his preaching and teaching. They need to know that the individual they are listening to can be trusted. David wrote in Psalm 25:21, "Let integrity and uprightness preserve me." And he prayed to the Lord in Psalm 41:12, "You uphold me in my integrity." That is constantly my prayer as well—for the Lord to never let me live before my family, before my church, before a watching world in any way that is divergent from what I preach and what I say I believe.

Integrity should mark all believers, but most of all, the one who has the most at stake—the mouthpiece, the spokesman, the model, the example, the leader.

In addition, not only do I want to maintain integrity in my own life, I want to be surrounded by people who have integrity. In Psalm 101:6 David looked at his kingdom, along with whom he wanted around him, and said, "He who walks in a blameless way is the one who will minister to me." In fact, the alternate reading of that psalm is, "He who walks in a way of integrity…" Integrity should mark all believers, but most of all, the one who has the most at stake—the mouthpiece, the spokesman, the model, the example, the leader.

Defining Integrity

The Hebrew word translated "integrity" means whole or complete. Every part of a believer's life must be in perfect order with every other part. The word is used for what is flawless, what is perfect, what is blameless, and what is consistent. Even the English word *integrity* comes from *integer*, which is a mathematical term meaning one. The dictionary would define *integer* as the quality of being undivided. A few synonyms for integrity would be *honesty* or *without hypocrisy* or *without duplicity*. In other words, you live with integrity when you haven't covered anything up. First Timothy 3 reminds us that if a man wants to be an elder, he must be blameless and above reproach. All too often today's church leaders are focused on ministry efforts and goals that are defined by courage, energy, enthusiasm, optimism, entrepreneurship, and imagination. But Scripture is far more concerned about integrity.

An Attack on Integrity

Now, having mentioned that, the most precious commodity that I have as a pastor is my personal relationship to Christ. Therein lies the integrity of my ministry. As soon as it becomes obvious to my own children, family, church, or the watching world that I'm something different than what I preach, all is lost. Yet it is difficult to try to defend your integrity against your critics. I have had many critics and I have had them for a long time, but with the Internet, they've gone interplanetary. My daughter went to work for *Grace to You* a few years ago. She thought everyone loved her father because she lived in a microcosm of this church. Her responsibility at *Grace to You* was to process the letters sent by mail. She was shocked by all the hate mail that came in against me and was so crushed by it that she began clandestinely answering all these people. She would write back, "You don't know my father. Stop saying these things about him."

The most challenging part of ministry is receiving false accusations of being unfaithful, unbiblical, or guilty of any other sin. I remember, when I began in ministry, saying to my father, "Dad, will you pray for me?" He responded, "I will pray for you and I'll pray for two things specifically— that God will protect you from sin, and that God will protect you from people who accuse you of sins you don't commit." My father knew that pastors need to be protected from false accusations. As a pastor, you will be maligned, and sometimes these enemies are very close. Sometimes they're on the church board, and this will make the attacks painful.

An Integrity Worth Defending

The first step to defending your integrity is to have an integrity that is worth defending. But even then, defending oneself is tricky business, because it is difficult to do it without seeming self-serving or self-centered. I don't like defending myself, but I also know that when unfounded, unwarranted, untrue accusations and criticisms come against me, they destroy people's trust in my ministry. False accusations cut me off from an opportunity to bring the truth to the people who are under my influence. A pastor protecting his integrity is a pastor protecting the flock he shepherds.

In 1 Corinthians 4:3, Paul wrote that it is a small thing what men say of him, because God brings the final verdict. And in one sense it is not about personal feelings, self-esteem, self-protection, or making sure you go through life blissfully, but about how the words of certain men affect your ministry opportunity. It hurts to have your ministry maligned because it cuts you off from the people who buy into those lies and you no longer have the opportunity to be a servant of the Lord to them. That is especially painful when it occurs in the church. This has happened at Grace Community Church, where in one fell swoop, more than 200 people left in a protest against me under the assault of a false accusation some years ago. But I learned that if you have a life worth defending, then you're caught in this very awkward position of having to defend yourself.

Persuading Men

If you find yourself in this position, then you're in good company with the apostle Paul. You could take just about any passage in 2 Corinthians and the text would eventually get you to the place of looking at how Paul viewed his ministry and how he dealt with others who questioned his integrity. More specifically, there are three words that stand out in 2 Corinthians 5:11: "we persuade men." What exactly was Paul persuading men to? Was he talking about eagerly being engaged in persuading people to believe the gospel? Because Paul does that in other places in Scripture—for example, we read in Acts 18:4 that Paul was reasoning in the synagogue in Corinth every Sabbath, trying to persuade Jews and Greeks. And in Acts 28:22 a group came to Paul, and he was trying to persuade them concerning Jesus, from both the Law of Moses and from the Prophets, from morning until evening (verse 23). Paul was persuasive when it came to the gospel.

Yet the reference in 2 Corinthians 5:11 is not about persuading people to believe the gospel. Rather, Paul wrote about persuading men about his own integrity, which was a key issue in 2 Corinthians. At this time, Paul was under a full-scale assault by false teachers in Corinth who were teaching a mangled mixture of Christianity, Judaism, and pagan religions. In their attempt to successfully teach these lies and fulfill their satanic agenda, these false teachers had to destroy that congregation's trust in the reigning teacher, Paul.

Consequently, Paul wrote to persuade the Corinthians of his own integrity, for it had been illegitimately assaulted. In chapter 1, he wrote about all the suffering he had endured. The false teachers claimed that Paul's suffering was due to divine judgment. But Paul reminded the church that though he was suffering, he was suffering for the sake of the gospel. In chapter 4, Paul stressed that this suffering was occurring so that he could comfort the church. He was even attacked about his honesty. His critics were saying, "You don't do what you say you're going to do. You said you were coming, and you didn't come." Paul responded by reminding the people in the church that he could only do what the Lord allowed him to do. The apostle had to defend his own integrity. Then the false teachers attacked his virtue, and he replied that he did not have a secret life of shame and that there was no other Paul.

The false teachers accused Paul of being proud and wanting to elevate himself, and he reminded the church that he was nothing more than a clay pot, an earthen vessel. The teachers questioned his openness, and he wrote back, "Our heart is opened wide" (6:11). He was accused of being in the ministry for sexual favors and money. He responded, "We wronged no one, we corrupted no one, we took advantage of no one" (7:2). They attacked his apostleship, as if it was illegitimate, and he reminded the people that he was not inferior to any apostle. They attacked his giftedness, saying that his persona and his speech were unimpressive and contemptible, and they even attacked his message. They hit him every way they could. Their accusations were flying all over the Corinthian church and they were landing on Paul to such a degree that Paul admitted that he was depressed (7:6). I've been there, and you've been there. We are looking at our life like Job and doing our best to walk the walk and to live what we preach. We hate to become defensive because we don't want to seem overly self-protective, but we still understand what is at stake.

As a result, "we persuade men" (5:11). This phrase unlocks the door to this little portion of Scripture and to how we defend our integrity. Paul used a plural pronoun because he was talking about himself, yet at the same time he was also strategically avoiding saying "I." The Greek word translated "persuade" is *peithomen*, the same term used in Galatians 1:10, in the negative sense, where it means to seek the favor of men. In Galatians, Paul did not care about seeking the favor of those who rejected the true gospel. But in 2 Corinthians he was on the opposite end—he was seeking a favorable response from the church because he was defending his own integrity.

Appealing to God

I speak to pastors who contact me to talk about the terrible assaults that are going on against them in their churches. My response is, "Defend yourself if you have a life worth defending." Likewise, Paul wanted the favor and the trust of his church. Note the phrase that follows "we persuade men"—"but we are made manifest to God" (5:11). As a leader, if you are going to say, "I want to persuade you of my integrity," then you are also going to have to say, "And God knows the truth about me." God is the one who knows our true spiritual condition and our heart. In these types of situations, we must be willing to gladly stand before God's court and take whatever discipline is deserved.

Another court that Paul appealed to was his own conscience. In 2 Corinthians 1:12 he wrote, "Our proud confidence is this: the testimony of our conscience, that in holiness and godly sincerity, not in fleshly wisdom but in the grace of God, we have conducted ourselves in the world, and especially toward you." No matter what was said against Paul, what accusations came his way, what slander was spoken, what book was written against him, his conscience was clear. Though some people were accusing Paul, his conscience was not. In chapter 1 Paul appealed to the court of his conscience, but in chapter 5 he went to even a higher court—God Himself, who knew the sincerity and integrity of the apostle's heart. Pastor, what peace will come to your soul when you can say, "God knows my heart."

In Acts 23:1, Paul mentioned that he had lived his life with a perfectly good conscience, and in Acts 24:16, he said he had done his best to maintain a blameless conscience. Now that is an integrity and life worth defending. It is only when one has a clear conscience and knows that by the grace of God he has lived in holiness and godly sincerity that he can rise to a legitimate defense of his integrity for the sake of the One he represents.

If there is any one thing that undergirds the teaching of the Word of God, it is the sincere integrity of the minister.

Reasons for Defending Your Integrity

The integrity of the messenger is a critical aspect of making the message acceptable. At the end of 2 Corinthians 5:11, Paul wrote, "I hope that we are made manifest also in your conscience." Paul wanted these people to trust him, to not have doubts about him, to not believe all the lies about him, to not listen to all the evil criticisms of the false teachers, and instead to listen to their own conscience. Paul was saying, "I trust your conscience more than I would trust those false teachers, because you belong to Christ and you know me personally. Your conscience has been formed by the truth of God, informed by the truth of God, and is operating under the influence of the Spirit of God." The evidence of Paul's sincerity was critical to the effect of his ministry. If there is any one thing that undergirds the teaching of the Word of God, it is the sincere integrity of the minister. Paul knew that and was willing to fight to defend himself.

Reverence for the Lord

Why is it important to defend your ministry and integrity? The *first* reason is a reverence for the Lord. Paul wrote, "For we must all appear before the judgment seat of Christ, so that each one may be recompensed for his deeds in the body, according to what he has done, whether good or bad" (verse 10). Paul then transitioned to this in verse 11: "Therefore, knowing the fear of the Lord, we persuade men." We are to have reverence and fear toward being examined by the Lord and the possibility that He would determine our deeds are "bad" (Greek, *phaulos*), which means worthless.

I suppose the strongest driving force in my life is reverence for the Lord. My view of God drives and compels me. It is my view of God that drives my view of Scripture. Paul wrote, "Knowing the fear of the Lord..." The Greek word translated fear is *phobos*, from which we get the word *phobia*. It is a strong word that can even be translated as "terror." However, Paul was not intending to speak of God as the One who judges and condemns. Rather, he was writing about the admiration, respect, and worship that the Lord excites in his soul—the compelling desire to worship Him, honor Him, and glorify Him.

One difficult aspect of being criticized is that it's disheartening to know there are people who think that I would do something that would bring shame on the name of Christ. The last thing I would ever want to do is dishonor the Lord. To know the fear of the Lord is the ultimate form of accountability. What controls the heart is a healthy fear of the Lord, or awe and reverence. Paul wrote that he knew this fear—the word "knowing" refers to a settled knowledge. Paul had the settled knowledge of God as a Lord to be adored, and his obedience stemmed from this proper knowledge of God.

We find the opposite response in Jonah, whom God commanded, "Go to Nineveh." Jonah's reply was, "I'm not going to Nineveh. I know the kind of God You are. You'll save those people." Sadly, a proper knowledge of God led Jonah to be disobedient. For Paul, however, this knowledge led to obedience. It is as if Paul was saying, "I know what kind of God I have. I love Him, I adore Him, and I want to glorify Him." Paul cared about his integrity because he cared about the name of Jesus being worshipped.

The apostle wanted nothing to undermine the truth of his faithfulness to the Christ he proclaimed. He certainly wanted to face the judgment seat of Christ and hear, "Well done, good and faithful servant." If his reputation was ruined, the Lord's name would be shamed, and his usefulness would be gone. His fruitfulness would be curtailed. Consequently, Paul lived in holiness and godly sincerity because he did not want God to be dishonored.

Concern for the Church

The *second* reason Paul defended his integrity was because of his concern for the church. We understand what happens to the church when integrity is shattered. Paul wrote, "We are not again commending ourselves to you but are giving you an occasion to be proud of us, so that you will have an answer for those who take pride in appearance and not in heart" (5:12). When Paul spoke about "those who take pride in appearance and not in heart," he was referring to the false teachers who were into works-based righteousness. False teachers always come along and take pride in appearance and not in heart. For them, it's all about looking good externally, because false religion can never change the heart.

As pastors, we want to live with integrity so that the church would be proud of us and defend us against false accusers. Paul realized it was necessary to defend himself because the false teachers were harming the church's confidence in him. He knew their attacks on his integrity would create discord, retard growth, and cripple the church's testimony. Paul's concern for his reputation was for the church's sake. He was not attempting to be newly vindicated; this was just an opportunity for the congregation to step up and demonstrate that they were proud of Paul by answering the critics. Yet apparently they did not do this.

In fact, the last time Paul made a visit to Corinth, someone in the church stood up and falsely accused him. And when no one defended him, he left with a broken heart. That's why Paul was hesitant about coming back. He did not know if he could stand the pain. The apostle was hoping these people would rally around their minister, rally around the truth that he taught, and take the initiative against the intruders.

I met a very prominent TV preacher on a flight one night from Chicago. He happened to be inebriated about half an hour into the flight, and when he saw me, he treated me with significant disdain. I responded, "This is interesting because I'm now in the process of writing a little article about you." A few days after I got back to Los Angeles, I received an envelope in the mail from him. It read, "Dear John: Thanks for the wonderful fellowship on the flight from Chicago…" He of course had written this letter so that if I brought up anything about his drinking, he could deny it. Along with the letter from him, he had attached about 12 other letters, all from different people praising him. We understand that it matters to be defended by people other than ourselves. But this defense did not work for me, because I was on the plane and saw the reality of his condition. In 2 Corinthians, Paul also did not want to write only a testimonial to himself, even though it was believable he did have integrity. He knew it is better when a congregation rises up to a pastor's defense.

The apostle wanted his Corinthian friends to boldly confront the enemies of the church and rise to protect their faithful minister and shepherd. Paul would prefer to "let another praise you, and not your own mouth" (Proverbs 27:2). He wrote that he and his fellow workers were giving the Corinthian believers "an occasion to be proud of us" (2 Corinthians 5:12). He wanted the church to boast of him, in the right sense of the word. They needed to take up his case. They needed to answer his detractors. They had all the information, because they had sat under his ministry for nearly two years. What else could Paul write that had not been already written and said?

That was the situation Jonathan Edwards found himself in as well. He had ministered for more than 20 years in one church and was a catalyst for the Great Awakening, but the church threw him out and spread the word against him so far and wide that he was reduced to ministering to a settlement of Indians. Spurgeon experienced this when the Baptist Union threw him out with an overwhelming vote that was seconded by his own brother, who was his assistant pastor. Paul understood that a minister has to defend himself for the sake of the strength and unity of the church.

Devotion to the Truth

The *third* reason we defend our integrity is for devotion to the truth. "If we are beside ourselves, it is for God; if we are of sound mind, it is for you" (2 Corinthians 5:13). Paul was not defending himself in a self-serving manner, but out of devotion to the people in the church and to God. "Beside ourselves" means to be out of one's mind. This entails that the people were calling Paul crazy, claiming he had lost his mind. But this same term is used to describe excitement and enthusiasm. Paul was saying, "If I appear over-the-top excited and enthusiastic, it's for God. If I am passionate and seem insane, there is a reason for it. I'm a fanatic about God and His truth."

How could Paul not be enthused, passionate, and zealous when what he did was all for God? For the divine truth that had been given to him and needed to be passed on to others so they could believe.

Next, Paul wrote, "And if we are of sound mind"—that is, if there are times when we are moderate, sober-minded, calm, cool, collected, meek, humble, and restrained—"it is for you." There's a part of a pastor that is passionate, zealous, and over the top. But there is also a part that is sober-minded, analytical, and careful in all the things he does and says. Paul was reasonable when he needed to be reasonable, and he was passionate when he couldn't contain his love for the truth and the God of that truth.

A Gratitude for Salvation

A *fourth* reason for defending integrity is a gratitude for salvation, or a gratitude for saving love. "For the love of Christ controls us" (5:14). Everything that Paul did was because of the fact that Christ's love controlled him. What had come into Paul's life took over him completely. He wrote, "For the love of Christ controls us, having concluded this, that one died for all, therefore all died; and He died for all, so that they who live might no longer live for themselves, but for Him who died and rose again on their behalf" (5:14-15).

Paul was defending his integrity because he was constrained to maintaining a place of effective ministry, usefulness, and believability. The apostle was willing to fight on account of Christ's great love for him. He knew that one way to show gratitude for that love was by giving himself in sacrificial ministry on behalf of the gospel. Pastor, do you love Christ enough to make all the sacrifices necessary to live a life of gratitude? To clarify, a life of gratitude is a life of holiness and godly sincerity that gives back in gratitude the integrity of ministry that pleases the Lord and says, "Thank You for Your unspeakable gift" (see 2 Corinthians 9:15).

Paul wanted to minister because "One died for all." This is one of the greatest theological statements you'll find anywhere in the epistles. Now let's get a little technical here by asking who fits into the category of "all." Fortunately, the word "all" is qualified in verse 14: "therefore all died." If you assume that "all" refers to all of humanity that has ever lived, then you are holding to a Universalist perspective. Do you believe everybody who has ever lived is going to heaven? If your answer is no, then you understand that Christ's atonement has limits.

The "all" whom Christ died for are those who believe in Him. He rose on their behalf only. The text itself tells us that this is a specific death, an act of substitution. Do not allow yourself to think that Jesus did the same thing on the cross for all the people in hell as He did for the people in heaven. That would mean He died for nobody in particular. Some people see Christ's death as a potential that is actualized when a person comes to believe in Jesus. But how can spiritually dead sinners activate a potential atonement? Jesus did not die a vague death; He died for all those who are His elect children. He said, "I am the good shepherd, and I know My own and My own know Me, even as the Father knows Me and I know the Father; and I lay down My life for the sheep" (John 10:14-15).

Paul had a heart of gratitude because he understood the actual atoning substitutionary death that Christ had died for him. It was this overwhelming reality—the fact that before he ever came into existence, God in His eternal and sovereign love had purposed that Jesus Christ would bear his sins in His own body on the cross—that led to Paul's gratitude.

Paul then wrote in verse 16, "Therefore from now on we recognize no one according to the flesh; even though we have known Christ according to the flesh, yet now we know Him in this way no longer." Paul, at one point, thought Jesus was a charlatan and a fraud. He would have been screaming, "Crucify Him" with everybody else in that crowd before Pilate. But because that was already history, he expressed his opposition to Jesus by persecuting Christians. Paul originally had a human view of Christ: "We have known Christ according to the flesh." Yet after his conversion, "We know Him in this way no longer." Paul's view was transformed. He was, as he said in verse 17, "A new creature; the old things passed away; behold, new things have come."

Defending Your Own Integrity

Paul was transformed through his faith in Christ and Christ's substitutionary atoning death on his behalf. This truth of the cross leads to an all-consuming gratitude for salvation that results in a defense of integrity. How could Paul not defend the nature of his new identity, which was purchased by the precious blood of Christ? Likewise, as a pastor, seek to possess an integrity that is worth defending, and defend it because the cross has made you a new creation.

Opposition and Hope

"The Most High is ruler over the realm of mankind
and bestows it on whomever He wishes."

Daniel 4:25

6

OPPOSITION AND HOPE

Mark Dever

Shepherds' Conference 2007

Daniel 1–6

Recently I was surprised by a publication that instructed Muslims about the correctness of killing Christians in Saudi Arabia. The book encouraged Muslims to fight their own personal jihad and work to expose what they see as an evil cabal controlling the American government.

As Christians, at least in the West, we feel more troubled and uncertain than we may have felt 30 years ago. At the very same time, there seems to be growing among us indigenous threats to our public ministries and liberties, as well as challenges to the free practice of the Christian faith in this land. There is the entrenched secularism of our elites, which dismisses the validity of Christianity and eats away at the residual cultural empathy that there is for the gospel. And there is also the innervating and exhausting reality of our unchallenged addiction to comfort amidst perilously growing material affluence.

With our ideas marginalized by the elites and with our eyelids growing heavy through the warm embrace of worldly ease, we find ourselves particularly unprepared to combat a fairly new phenomenon in this country—the phenomenon of legal intolerance toward an exclusive faith like Christianity. Hate crimes, which are detestable things, are increasingly described as the inevitable result of hate speech. Speech that others deem as incitement to violence, even nonphysical violence, is increasingly regarded as socially disruptive and wrong. Condemnations of homosexuality are taken to be incitements to personal violence against people. The ground is being prepared at local, state, and federal levels alike to make statements decrying homosexuality or even statements denying the truth of other religions be categorized as hate speech.

In short, any statements that might prove inflammatory are to be classified as illegal. Christians who have for so long dominated the scene in America, and at least have been widely tolerated in the West, are now beginning to face the prospect of living in a world that does not so easily accept our freedoms to make certain claims and denials. As pastors, we are on the front line of this change, and if you don't realize that now, you will within the next few years.

What do we do when we're told that it's illegal to say another religion is false or homosexuality is wrong? You may say, "Well, Mark, that's on your mind because you're a pastor on Capitol Hill in Washington, DC. A third of your congregation is made up of lawyers." Friend, I wish that was the only reason we should think about this, but there are already many places around the world where these threats are realized. We have to remember that many of our brothers and sisters this very day are facing oppression, whether from Latin American Roman Catholics, Indian Hindu nationalists, Muslims, communists, or secularists. It's fair to say that even while we enjoy the freedom of meeting in this country, there is no such freedom for Christians in many other places around the world.

But what if our laws here in America become like the laws of most nations around the world today? What if there were more public intolerance toward our faith that makes it difficult to have a public meeting? What should we do?

The Example of Daniel

We find our answer in the Old Testament, and there are few portions of the Bible that are as instructive for us in this matter as the book of Daniel. Most Christians are familiar with at least the first half of this book, since it is full of famous stories regularly mined by parents who want to prevent their kids from going with the crowd. In chapter 1, Daniel stood up for his diet. In chapters 2 through 6 he stood up for his faith. These chapters are full of human drama and valor in the face of danger, truth in response to threats, uncompromising faithfulness in places full of the temptations of power and wealth. In these biographical chapters of Daniel, you have two sieges, four kings, and lots of dreams and visions. The rest of the book, chapters 7 through 12, is no longer a story of Daniel, but focuses on Daniel reporting about his visions. Here we will focus on the first six chapters.

As vivid as Daniel's story is, it is often misunderstood. It's often interpreted and applied as a religious "how to succeed" manual. Certainly there is much we can learn from Daniel's example. In chapter 1, Jerusalem was besieged by the most powerful king in the ancient Near East, the Babylonian emperor Nebuchadnezzar. As a young man, perhaps even a teenager, Daniel was taken into captivity. Once in Babylon, he was selected for a special program so he could be trained as an advisor to the king. He was successful and was treated with favor by those in charge. He was allowed to eat his own food so that he wouldn't become ceremonially unclean according to his own religion, and he gained great knowledge and understanding.

In chapter 2, King Nebuchadnezzar made an impossible demand of his wise men regarding a vision that he'd had. It was Daniel alone who was able to describe the vision and interpret it for the king. The rest of the story in these first six chapters continues in the same vein, with Daniel being both outstandingly faithful and a model of prosperity at the same time. Outstandingly faithful as he faced real opposition, and yet he always prospered.

The Purpose of Daniel

Of course this isn't just a story about Daniel. If you look back to Daniel 1:2, you see that Nebuchadnezzar's conquest of Jerusalem was possible because God allowed it. Though it may seem like Judah's God had been defeated, this verse makes it clear that it was the Lord who delivered Jerusalem into the hands of the Babylonians. And the official who showed favor to Daniel's dietary restriction was provoked by God (verse 9). As for Daniel gaining understanding, we see that it was God who gave him knowledge and wisdom (verse 17). Daniel served in the court as a wise man and advisor for almost 70 years after he was deported to Babylon. That's longer than Winston Churchill's public career, and that too was a result of God's favor. As for Daniel interpreting Nebuchadnezzar's dream, we read that the mystery was revealed to Daniel in a vision that came from God. Even the purpose of the dream and its interpretation was to show to Nebuchadnezzar that his power came from God: "The God of heaven has given [you] the kingdom, the power, the strength and the glory" (2:37-38).

We don't know exactly when this vision came to Nebuchadnezzar. And we see that the king would not tell the astrologers what his dream was, because if he had told them, then he wouldn't know if he should trust their interpretation. However, the astrologers were against Nebuchadnezzar's demand. We read in Daniel 2:10, "There is not a man on earth who could declare the matter for the king, inasmuch as no great king or ruler has ever asked anything like this of any magician, conjurer or Chaldean." They were right—only the true God could reveal this vision and its meaning.

Daniel accepted this impossible task because he knew God was able.

> The king said to Daniel, whose name was Belteshazzar, "Are you able to make known to me the dream which I have seen and its interpretation?" Daniel answered before the king and said, "As for the mystery about which the king has inquired, neither wise men, conjurers, magicians nor diviners are able to declare it to the king. However, there is a God in heaven who reveals mysteries, and He has made known to King Nebuchadnezzar what will take place in the latter days" (Daniel 2:26-28).

The message of this book is that God causes His faithful to survive, and that's a message pastors need to hear.

Surely we, along with all the readers of this story for the last millennia, must admire Daniel's courage and his willingness to stand alone for the truth. But is this the point of these stories in Daniel? I want us to look at Daniel as an example, but in a way that's different than what is often taught in Sunday school. I want to look at Daniel more as an example of what God does with faith. The message of this book is that God causes His faithful to survive, and that's a message pastors need to hear. We'll look at three lessons we can learn from the first six chapters of Daniel.

Lessons to Learn from Daniel

God Is Our Hope

The first lesson we must learn is that God is our only hope. The book of Daniel exposes the myth of the godless world that we are left in this world without hope. Whether you are a refugee from a defeated nation, a religious minority under an unjust sentence of death, have your friends persecuted and executed, are called to speak difficult things to people above you and stationed in power, or you are a pastor with your back against the wall, you still have hope, and it is in God, who is the true sovereign of the world. You do not stand at the mercy of an election or legislation, for God is the one who is sovereign.

God's faithfulness is the explanation for Daniel's survival and prosperity. All throughout the book of Daniel, God is shown to be powerful and in control. We certainly see God's power in the wonderful story about Shadrach, Meshach, and Abednego. We read their response to Nebuchadnezzar in Daniel 3:17: "If it be so, our God whom we serve is able to deliver us from the furnace of blazing fire; and He will deliver us out of your hand, O king." Even Nebuchadnezzar referred to God as the "Most High" (verse 26). In verse 28 we read the king's proclamation, "Blessed be to the God of Shadrach, Meshach and Abednego who has sent His angel and delivered His servants who put their trust in Him, violating the king's command, and yielded up their bodies so as not to serve or worship any god except their own God." The central feature of this book, then, is not Daniel's faithfulness, but God's faithfulness. If you understand this truth, then it will be wonderful news to your soul.

Before Nebuchadnezzar condemned Shadrach, Meshach, and Abednego, he seems to have entirely forgotten the lessons he had learned earlier when he had his troublesome dream. He blustered in verse 15, "What god is there who can deliver you out of my hands?" Then we have that amazing response we just read in Daniel 3:16-18—Shadrach, Meshach, and Abednego were faithful to God and trusted Him completely. Theirs was a confident, trusting, humble, and joyful statement that persecuted Christians ought to say to their persecutors. We know our God is sovereign, and He may exercise His sovereignty in ways that we don't understand right now, but even if He chooses not to save us, He is a wise and good God, and we can trust Him.

Daniel's friends made evident the confidence that we as Christians are to have. They were sentenced to a fiery death: "Then Nebuchadnezzar was filled with wrath, and his facial expression was altered toward Shadrach, Meshach and Abednego. He answered by giving orders to heat the furnace seven times more than it was usually heated" (3:19). The furnace was so hot that the flames killed the men who tied up and put Shadrach, Meshach, and Abednego into the furnace. There, in that blazing furnace, the very place where earthly power like Nebuchadnezzar's would seem to be at its absolute height, Nebuchadnezzar saw the limits of his power. His earthly power was unmasked by the sovereign God, in whose hand is all power. Nebuchadnezzar was amazed, for in this place that he meant to show his power, instead, he found out who was the real ruler of the world. And after he saw the power of God, he praised the true God.

Yet even this conviction eventually faded away. In chapter 4, we see that the king's pride had grown again. The historical setting seems to be near the end of Nebuchadnezzar's reign. Commentators speculate that it was around 570 BC, when most of his building projects would have been finished, and it was then that Nebuchadnezzar provided an account of the Lord humbling him. The king said, "It has seemed good to me to declare the signs and wonders which the Most High God has done for me. How great are His signs and how mighty are His wonders! His kingdom is an everlasting kingdom and His dominion is from generation to generation" (verses 2-3). Then in verse 17: "The Most High is ruler over the realm of mankind, and bestows it on whom He wishes and sets over it the lowliest of men." Daniel echoed this statement in verse 25: "The Most High is ruler over the realm of mankind and bestows it on whomever He wishes." Nebuchadnezzar closed the chapter by saying, "I blessed the Most High and praised and honored Him who lives forever; for His dominion is an everlasting dominion, and His kingdom endures from generation to generation" (verse 34). Nebuchadnezzar offered praise to the most high.

You might think that because you're not the emperor of a great empire, but rather, the pastor of a small church, that pride cannot reside in your own heart. Not true. Nebuchadnezzar is proud here. He may have been able to capture Jerusalem, but Jerusalem's God was still unassailably sovereign over him, even in the capture. Nebuchadnezzar may have had a long reign, but God has a reign that will never end. Nebuchadnezzar may have built one of the great wonders of the ancient world, but it was God who made the world.

It is simply false and distorting when we begin thinking of ourselves in mighty ways because we are not our own best hope—God is! There is no Utopia in this fallen world. There is hope for eternity through the life, death, and resurrection of our Lord Jesus Christ. Through Christ, God becomes our hope just as He has been the hope and help of others. I'm reminded of the letter that Adoniram Judson wrote to Luther Rice when he was trying to raise money for Christian missions. Judson was overseas, and Rice was getting complaints about Judson's missionary work being hopeless and pointless. Judson wrote, "If they ask again, 'What prospect of ultimate success is there?' Tell them, 'As much as there is in almighty and faithful God, who will perform His promises, and no more.'"

Friend, the only hope we have today isn't our integrity, hard work, fortune, cleverness, or even courage. Our only hope is the same as Daniel's—God Himself. This book is here to remind us that only God can give us the faith and faithfulness we need. It's when we have exhausted our own strength that we are then in the perfect place to trust the Lord. Like that fiery furnace that Shadrach, Meshach, and Abednego went through or that deacons meeting you just went through, remember, you are a child of God. Do not despair, but realize that God is building a stage upon to which make clear His power and His faithfulness. Please remember that in your ministries. And remember to teach this to your people and deconstruct their false and deceptive hopes. Liberate them from lies and serve them by emancipating them from error with the message of these chapters, which tell us that God is our only hope.

You Can Survive Opposition

A second lesson we learn in Daniel 1–6 is that you can survive opposition. Daniel's survival is meant to be an inspiration to us, more than just a "how-to" instruction guide. Daniel is to be a motivation for the hope that we need. Also, it's amazing to see Daniel survive as long as he did! The kings he served had such great power—they were absolute monarchs, unchecked by any parliament or popularity, by press or poll. Yet Daniel survived the king that had destroyed his native city, carried him to exile, and even sentenced him to death.

In chapter 5 we see Daniel, probably the only survivor in the king's court, still within the orbit of the king in 539 BC, only it's clear that the king has changed. The king is now Belshazzar, who was shaken when he saw the hand that wrote a message on the wall. Belshazzar promised Daniel that if he could properly interpret the writing, then he would make him the third ruler in the kingdom. The reason for the third position was because the Babylonian emperor was Nabonidus, and Belshazzar was his son. Because Nabonidus was still alive, Belshazzar was considered number two in the kingdom. So by offering Daniel the third place in the kingdom, Belshazzar was offering Daniel the highest place available.

By this time Daniel was nearing his eighties. And he responded with the courage that approaching death gives: "Keep your gifts for yourself or give your rewards to someone else" (5:17). He then confronted the king:

> Yet you, his son, Belshazzar, have not humbled your heart, even though you knew all this, but you have exalted yourself against the Lord of heaven; and they have brought the vessels of His house before you, and you and your nobles, your wives and your concubines have been drinking wine from them; and you have praised the gods of silver and gold, of bronze, iron, wood and stone, which do not see, hear or understand. But the God in whose hand are your life-breath and all your ways, you have not glorified (verses 22-23).

Daniel then explained the writing on the wall, which was an indictment from the Lord: "This is the interpretation of the message: 'MENĒ'—God has numbered your kingdom and put an end to it. 'TEKĒL'—you have been weighed on the scales and found deficient. 'PERĒS'—your kingdom has been divided and given over to the Medes and Persians" (5:26-28). What is most amazing of all is that after this took place, Daniel prospered again. He had taken unusual risk to speak honestly to the king. And later that night, it wasn't Daniel who was slain; it was Belshazzar. We read in Daniel 5:30, "That same night Belshazzar the Chaldean king was slain." Darius the Mede took his place. Even though the Babylonian Empire had come to an end, Daniel once again survived—not only an emperor, but a whole empire.

Let's treasure the gospel and let's resolve afresh to hold out the good news of Jesus Christ around us, because this is how we will survive in this world and the next.

As a pastor, do you not see from this that there are no worldly circumstances that you will face that should ever drain your hope dry? All opposition to God's people, whether in this life or the next, will end. Therefore, let us labor to keep our hope in the gospel. Let's try to evacuate our hopes from every place else they may be, and put them in the gospel. When we keep our hopes on earthly matters, we keep them at our peril. They're either dashed, or worse than that, they appear to succeed, and so distract us. Jesus said, "Where your treasure is, there your heart will be also" (Luke 12:34). Let's treasure the gospel and let's resolve afresh to hold out the good news of Jesus Christ around us, because this is how we will survive in this world and the next.

Opposition Will Come

The third lesson is that you will face opposition. The book of Daniel exposes the myth that we live in an amoral world. In fact, the world is so fallen that it is normal for the godly to face opposition, and God's dealings with Daniel remind us of this reality. Pastor, wake up! You will face opposition. You don't hear this from evangelical pulpits, or in churches in the United States. Sometimes I fear that Christians are more like used car salesmen when it comes to the faith. They point out the good, cover up the difficult points, and do not sound like Jesus in the gospels or the apostles in Acts.

Daniel continued to face persecution even in the final years of his life. The man had survived three kings, and still faced opposition. It isn't clear when exactly Daniel died, but the events of chapter 6 must have taken place near the end of his life. It was at this time that the Babylonian Empire had fallen, but Daniel continued to prosper. We read in Daniel 6:1-2, "It seemed good to Darius to appoint 120 satraps over the kingdom, that they would be in charge of the whole kingdom, and over them three commissioners (of whom Daniel was one)." It's a whole different empire, and yet Daniel was still on top. Verse 3 continues, "Then this Daniel began distinguishing himself among the commissioners and satraps because he possessed an extraordinary spirit, and the king planned to appoint him over the entire kingdom." Daniel is in his seventies or older, and the king planned to set him over the whole kingdom.

But as is so often the case, there were unprincipled men who were willing to challenge Daniel and harm him. Daniel 6:5 reveals their thinking: "We will not find any ground of accusation against this Daniel unless we find it against him with regard to the law of his God." And the same still happens today. We must understand that we live in a fallen world and cannot expect a Utopia or perfect government. Though virtue may prevent us from being persecuted for doing wrong and it is commendable to work up our courage and integrity as Daniel did, the fact we are righteous is no guarantee that we will avoid trials.

This generation of evangelical ministers is called to tar the Ark before the flood of God's judgment comes upon our land. You are to teach believers that they will face opposition in a fallen world. Don't sell people lying nostrums in order to create apparent prosperity in your church. You are called to teach your people about the fall and the implications of the fall. Pastors who are from other places in the world will be lovingly bemused that this is news or that anyone could be surprised by this because they've lived under far more difficult circumstances.

The liberty and material prosperity in America, though it has been an obvious blessing from God, has crippled the church in some ways. We must prepare ourselves by reading the book of Daniel, understanding that even the most virtuous will face opposition. The fallen world is so bent that when God Himself appeared in the flesh, He was opposed, persecuted, and crucified. But there is good news: If you go on to read the rest of Daniel and the visions in chapters 7–12, you'll see that ultimately, God wins.

A consistent element of these visions is that the saints are under attack in this world. For example, we read in Daniel 7:21, "I kept looking, and that horn was waging war with the saints and overpowering them." Moreover, "He will speak out against the Most High and wear down the saints of the Highest One" (7:25). Chapter 8 reveals this about suffering for God's people:

> It grew up to the host of heaven and caused some of the host and some of the stars to fall to the earth, and it trampled them down. It even magnified itself to be equal with the Commander of the host; and it removed the regular sacrifice from Him, and the place of His sanctuary was thrown down. And on account of transgression the host will be given over to the horn along with the regular sacrifice; and it will fling truth to the ground and perform its will and prosper. Then I heard a holy one speaking, and another holy one said to that particular one who was speaking, "How long will the vision about the regular sacrifice apply, while the transgression causes horror, so as to allow both the holy place and the host to be trampled?" He said to me, "For 2,300 evenings and mornings; then the holy place will be properly restored" (10-14).

The interpretation is found in verses 24-25:

> His power will be mighty, but not by his own power, and he will destroy to an extraordinary degree and prosper and perform his will; he will destroy mighty men and the holy people. And through his shrewdness he will cause deceit to succeed by his influence; and he will magnify himself in his heart, and he

will destroy many while they are at ease. He will even oppose the Prince of princes, but he will be broken without human agency.

From this exile that God's people were enduring to the various trials that are mentioned in Daniel 9, it is clear that being the people of God won't be a walk in the park. Mighty rulers will show favor to those who forsake God. Temptations and troubles will multiply. Pressure will be brought to bear on those who have been faithful to God, and many will lose their lives. In Daniel 12:7 we read, "They finish shattering the power of the holy people." My intent is not to get into the particular eschatology of these verses because we can understand them to refer to a final tribulation. What is evident here is that from the cross of Christ until His return, the world will be at enmity with God.

By our very nature, we don't like and want to avoid trials. Yet real Christianity doesn't presume to deliver from suffering in the present moment. You will have trials as a Christian, and we see from the book of Acts that the early Christians did so regularly. Jesus said, "Remember the word that I said to you, 'A slave is not greater than his master.' If they persecuted Me, they will also persecute you" (John 15:20). Our present situation of almost no visible persecution is actually unusual in the history of Christianity, even among the Christians who live in other parts of the world today. So I warn you to not get comfortable. Worldly comfort only serves to make cavities in our souls, to weaken us, to misguide us, and to misdirect our efforts.

Some think that maneuvering correctly in politics can help Christianity avoid suffering. While politics is a noble calling, and many ills have been alleviated by this noble public work, in our fallen world, Christian politicians will no more be able to eliminate persecution than Christian doctors will be able to eliminate death. We are in a fallen world at enmity with God, and our brothers and sisters in politics cannot promise less persecution. The day we don't suffer for following Christ is an odd day. Therefore, we are not to run away from pain and suffering, but to walk with God through those trying times and let Him teach us how to turn each bit of suffering into positive learning about the depths of God's love.

I guarantee that Shadrach, Meshach, and Abednego had more confidence in God the night after they were thrown into the fiery furnace. Likewise, cancer, surgery, unemployment, death, bereavement, and broken relationships will help an individual see something of the riches that God has committed toward strengthening the believer's faith. Persecution and trials are platforms that God has built to show His power, sufficiency, and loving-kindness toward His people.

Your congregation is a treasury of sufferings, from arthritis to loneliness, from bereavement to confusion. And God allows you to be a living testimony about having Him, trusting Him, and knowing that being His child is better than having happy marriages, or never-ending earthly friendships, or even legal toleration of Christians. Knowing Christ is better than all else.

A commitment to God's glory above our own will normally bring suffering in this world. Peter wrote,

> If when you do what is right and suffer for it you patiently endure it, this finds favor with God. For you have been called for this purpose, since Christ also suffered for you, leaving you an example for you to follow in His steps, who committed no sin, nor was any deceit found in His mouth; and while being reviled, He did not revile in return; while suffering, He uttered no threats, but kept entrusting Himself to Him who judges righteously (1 Peter 2:20-23).

Is this what is expected when someone becomes a Christian? Is this what is expected when someone goes into the ministry? It is vital to consider carefully your expectations, because wrong expectations are a danger to souls. Let your expectations be shaped by what God promises in His Word. Consider all the trials Daniel faced even though he was a blessed man. The way you prepare for trials is by growing in your love for Christ.

Although we want to live in such way that people around us like us, we cannot expect that this will happen. Especially if the courts uphold certain kinds of hate speech legislation, we can't be too surprised if pastors will be charged with public crimes the way they have been in Canada, Australia, Norway, England, and elsewhere for doing nothing other than preaching the Bible. If there are individuals in the pastorate who are expecting worldly prosperity, then they should get out now before they're publicly and eternally embarrassed. However, we will endure all circumstances when we have found something that we love more than this world's praises and prosperity.

An Example of Suffering

I had the joy of listening to J. Smith recently in Manhattan. J. Smith is an American evangelist who lives in London and ministers to Muslims. He goes to Hyde Park Corner to debate Muslims and stands up on a soapbox to declare the truth. He shared with us about how some of the individuals who were found guilty in the London subway bombings were familiar faces who were among the crowds that he regularly spoke to at Hyde Park Corner. After the bombing, he asked the Muslims who had gathered near him, "How many of you think what these guys did was a good thing?" About 30 hands went up. He then said, "How many of you want to do this yourself?" About 15 hands went up. J. Smith then told our gathering, "We Christians should all be willing to be killed. My wife knows that someday I'll be killed because of the work I do." Friend, can you imagine having that kind of mind-set? I believe Daniel had that kind of mind-set. And I hope you have that kind of mind-set as well—that you are willing to endure opposition faithfully because you possess the ultimate hope of spending eternity with your Savior.

PRAYER

Lord, we thank You for Your example of enduring persecution. Even more, Lord, we thank You for Your being persecuted for us and enduring the wrath we deserve. We know we'll never experience the full extent of persecution we deserve because of Your kindness and amazing love to us in Christ. We pray that You would give us strength, educate our hearts, and inflame our lives with love for You above all things. We pray in Jesus' name, Amen.

THE LEADER AND HIS FLOCK

"Shepherd the flock of God among you,
exercising oversight not under compulsion,
but voluntarily, according to the will of God."

1 PETER 5:2

7

THE LEADER AND HIS FLOCK

Rick Holland

Shepherds' Conference 2011

1 Peter 5:1-4

First Peter 5:1-4 is familiar territory to anyone who is in ministry. In four simple verses, we get Pastoral Theology 101 all the way to the PhD, and we learn what it means to be a pastor, a leader, an overseer, and a shepherd:

> Therefore, I exhort the elders among you, as your fellow elder and witness of the sufferings of Christ, and a partaker also of the glory that is to be revealed, shepherd the flock of God among you, exercising oversight not under compulsion, but voluntarily, according to the will of God; and not for sordid gain, but with eagerness; nor yet as lording it over those allotted to your charge, but proving to be examples to the flock. And when the Chief Shepherd appears, you will receive the unfading crown of glory.

The Imagery of Sheep and Shepherds

The Bible is a zoo. It is full of animals and it should be, because the variety of animals speaks to the creativity of our Lord and Savior, Jesus, the agent of creation. The Bible mentions over 70 types of animals. The Old Testament contains 180 words to reference animals, while the New

Testament has about 50 words. There are clean and unclean animals, domesticated animals and wild beasts. There are cattle, goats, horses, camels, donkeys, pigs, dogs, snakes, frogs, bears, leopards, lions, foxes, jackals, wolves, fish, sparrows, eagles, vultures, worms, caterpillars, locusts, and even leviathans and behemoths.

Of all the animals, the sheep is the most frequently mentioned in the Bible, with more than 400 references. This is for good reason—sheep were a central part of the economy of Israel. They were raised for milk, meat, and wool. Sheep were also a central part of the sacrificial system. Because they were so essential, there also had to be shepherds. And if you want to comprehend the Bible's figurative references for shepherding people, then understanding the job of a shepherd in the ancient Near East is vital.

The conditions and the practices of shepherds back then were far different from what they are today. There were no fences, and the sheep could not be left by themselves inside an enclosure. Thus the sheep were completely dependent on their shepherds, who were responsible for protecting their flock against predators, sheltering them from threatening heat and cold, and leading them to pastures where they could feed and graze. In short, the shepherd was a provider, a protector, a guide, and an authority. Above all, the shepherd was a constant companion to his sheep.

Though shepherds were vital, they were not an esteemed part of the populace in Bible times. They were viewed as an odd sort because they lived nomadic lives in the wilderness. Their sole purpose was the care of their flock. They were hard-working blue-collar men. Yet these men were also special and respected at a certain level. Everyone knew that the welfare of the sheep, as well as the welfare of the sacrificial system itself, was due to the faithfulness of these shepherds.

This lesson on sheep husbandry is necessary because understanding the task of a shepherd is essential to grasping the pastoral imperative before us in 1 Peter 5:1-4. In verse 2, Peter instructed spiritual leaders to "shepherd the flock of God." The simple command is to be a shepherd and to shepherd the flock of God. Most dictionaries and encyclopedias that I consulted about shepherding made mention of the stupidity of sheep. Sheep don't survive very well unless they are protected. If they are left to themselves or subjected to even the smallest predator, they will not survive.

Sheep can't find their way back to a fold even when it's within sight. Some have witnessed sheep running off a cliff simply because they were mimicking other sheep.

Therefore, as we look at this familiar text, it's too easy to focus on the people we shepherd as lacking intelligence, being dependent, or being prone to wander. It's too easy to forget something very important: *We are sheep too.* When a man becomes a pastor, he does not become an undershepherd for God; rather, he becomes a sheepdog. For the term *undershepherd* is too much of a compliment. As pastors, we are the sheepdogs God sends out into the pasture to round up and care for His flock. We are those "unintelligent" and "dependent" sheep as well.

God is the ultimate shepherd of His people, but He has graciously called us to help with this work.

God's purpose for pastoral ministry is illustrated in the image of a shepherd. It's a metaphor he uses more than any other illustration in the Bible concerning spiritual oversight. In Jeremiah 3:15, the prophet lays this foundation by saying, "I will give you shepherds after My own heart." God is talking about that great day when the Messiah establishes His kingdom. How will we know these shepherds are after God's own heart? The next phrase tells us: "who will feed you on knowledge and understanding." God's standard of shepherding is a shepherd who is after His own heart. This passage provides the lens through which to view other passages about shepherding—the faithful shepherd looks to God his Shepherd and shepherds like God does. God is the ultimate shepherd of His people, but He has graciously called us to help with this work.

The Realities of Pastoral Ministry

In 1 Peter 5:1-4, Peter shows us what it means to be a shepherd-leader. Let me warn you: This is not for the fainthearted. Pastoral ministry is not for wimps. Pastoral ministry is not a social alternative to another job in the world. It's one of the most difficult, rigorous, painstaking, and crushing endeavors any human can undertake. This passage is about promoting the Great Shepherd while diminishing our role as shepherds.

In this passage, we observe three sobering realities of pastoral ministry, with the first one being...

Pastoral Ministry Is a Serious Responsibility

In verse 1 we read, "Therefore, I exhort the elders among you, as your fellow elder and witness of the sufferings of Christ, and a partaker also of the glory that is to be revealed..." Peter's exhortation is very specific, as it targets the elders. The term "elder" literally means someone who's older. However, when you study the semantic domain of this word and its usage in Jewish society, an "elder" was either senior in age or senior in experience. Sometimes there were younger men who were more senior in experience than older men. Someone once said, "It doesn't matter how long you've been in the canoe that determines how far you've gone across the lake, but how hard you've been pulling on the oars." There are younger men in ministry who pull very hard on the oars.

Three terms in this passage triangulate the vision and the responsibilities of a church leader—overseer, pastor, and elder. Verse 1 employs "elder" from the Greek term *presbuteros,* whereas verse 2 uses the verbal form of the Greek term *poimanate,* which means "shepherd" or "pastor," and the Greek word *episkopos,* which means "to exercise oversight." These three titles describe the office of an elder, who must be mature, wise, and has a heart and an ability to guide.

These three titles do not describe different kinds of men, nor different offices or roles, but characteristics that must converge in a spiritual leader. It is important to mention that though this passage references an office clearly outlined in the pastoral letters (1–2 Timothy and Titus), there are people who perform "overseeing" pastoral work as an extension of God's love for His flock without ever occupying a formal office. Paul had a similar understanding of these three terms. In Acts 20:17-28, he deployed the same three words—pastor, overseer, and elder—synonymously when he spoke to the elders at Ephesus. This signifies he was talking about a single office.

Peter wrote his first epistle to a group of believers whose lives were threatened because of their faith. And there are places in the world today where this experience is the reality for Christians. I have never suffered persecution that threatened my life. I've never been in a prayer meeting interrupted by a knock on the door and feared that Nero's guards had come to arrest me and take me to the lions. But that is the cultural context in which Peter's readers lived.

A noteworthy feature of Peter's letter is that instead of encouraging his readers with temporal comfort amidst persecution, he stressed that comfort would come at death. And until then, they were to be faithful. But if his emphasis was on faithfulness amidst persecution, then why did he shift to a discussion about elders at the close of his letter? Peter wanted to ensure that as the recipients encountered persecution and prosecution, someone was overseeing their lives, helping them have the proper perspective, and calling them to obedience. Persecution was no excuse for disobedience. Peter also wanted to make sure that the elders and pastors did not shrink away from shepherding people because of the oppression they might incur. After all, to be a pastor during this period was to make oneself a larger target for persecution.

That is why Peter began with the admonition to recognize the serious nature of ministry. Verse 1 begins with "therefore," which reverts the reader back to 1 Peter 4:17-18, where "judgment" is said to "begin with the household of God." Therefore, the strictest judgment and weight is on the leaders who are developing the maturity of the house of God. In addition, this verse contains the most extensive self-description of Peter in the epistle—"I'm your fellow elder and witness of the sufferings of Christ." Peter chose to identify himself not with an apostolic business card, but as a fellow elder: "I'm just like you. I'm a fellow elder. I'm a fellow overseer. I'm a fellow pastor." The bottom line? Peter was not asking the elders and pastors to do anything that he was not willing to do. Suffering exists for spiritual leaders too, and Peter understood their fears, temptations, and responsibilities. There's an important principle here: It's always the spiritual leaders who bear the brunt of persecution first. Peter embraced God's call on his own life as a leader in a church, a calling that would eventually lead to his martyrdom in Rome. And he was not asking other leaders to do anything that he was not doing himself.

Interestingly enough, Peter wrote that he was a "witness" of Christ's sufferings. Some scholars conclude from this that the author of this epistle cannot be Peter because Peter wasn't present at the cross. But how do we know Peter wasn't observing the cross from a distance? Though we have no evidence that he was present, neither do we have evidence that he was not. Tom Schreiner writes, "Peter did observe Christ in His ministry. He saw the opposition mount against Him, was present when He was arrested, and may have found his way to the cross even after denying Him."[1] Maybe, maybe not, but there's no reason to use this phrase to doubt that Peter wrote this epistle. Peter did witness the outcome of Christ's suffering.

The main point here is to beware. To take on the position and responsibility of spiritual leadership is to make yourself vulnerable to the same forces that killed Jesus. Think that through for a moment. If we take Peter seriously, to be a spiritual leader is to submit ourselves as vulnerable participants in and against those same principalities that were at war to put Christ on the cross. Not only the demonic forces, but also those who hate the morality of our God and the glory of our Savior Himself. And so Peter charges us to recognize that we have a serious responsibility.

Pastoral Ministry Is a Delegated Responsibility

In verses 2 and 3, Peter presented the second sobering reality of pastoral ministry: It is a delegated responsibility. After the resurrection, Peter had an unforgettable interview with the risen Lord on the shore of the Sea of Galilee. The same Peter who cut off a person's ear, ran for his life after the crucifixion, and went back to Galilee to fish once again now had an opportunity to converse with Jesus. We read in John 21:15, "When they had finished breakfast, Jesus said to Simon Peter, 'Simon, son of John, do you love me more than these?'" Peter must have choked on his fish as he heard Jesus' words. Jesus asked again, "'Simon, son of John, do you love me?' He said to Him, 'Yes, Lord; You know that I love You.' He said to him, 'Shepherd My sheep'" (verse 16). Once again the same verb appears that is translated "to shepherd the sheep." He said to him the third time,

"'Simon, son of John, do you love me?' Peter was grieved because He said to him the third time, 'Do you love me?' And he said to Him, 'Lord, You know all things; You know that I love You.' Jesus said to him, 'Tend My sheep'" (verse 17).

In most of the books that examine this passage and in most of the sermons I have heard on this text, the emphasis has been placed on why there are different Greek words used for love. I have done that as well. But may I suggest to you that's not the point? There's a repeated imperative that should be noted: "If you love Me, then pastor people." The point is to tend to the Lord's flock, to feed His sheep, and to pastor His people. Don't get lost in the debate over love: get busy about the work of tending the flock.

Jesus' command to shepherd is an interesting exhortation because it's something that we are to both do and be. Ephesians 4:11 says, "He gave some as apostles, and some as prophets, and some as evangelists, and some as pastors." The final word in the Greek text of that verse is the same word translated as "shepherd." C.H. Spurgeon said, "With all His maturity and firmness, the spiritual Father is full of tenderness and manifests an intense love for the souls of men."[2] Spurgeon continued that this pastor "was born on purpose to care for other people and his heart cannot rest until it is full of such care."[3]

According to Ephesians 4:11, pastoring people is more than something you do. It defines you. We were "born on purpose" to care for others. And to care for others is always a self-denying fight against our own flesh. As we investigate 1 Peter chapter 5, the first phrase in verse 2 is the most important in the entire passage. We find in it an impossible responsibility: to shepherd the church which is "the flock of God." Peter didn't say, "Shepherd your flock." He said, "Shepherd the flock of God among you." This is God's flock, not ours. These sheep are God's lambs. He commands us to tend them for Him, to pastor them for Him, and to care for them because they belong to Him.

Also, notice that the ministry is localized—this flock is "among you." Peter is not talking about the Internet or blogosphere. I'm thankful for websites and blogs; I read some daily and they are very helpful. However, we have to be careful not to neglect the local flock by engaging with others in the blogosphere, which is not the church.

Peter continued by challenging shepherds to be "exercising oversight." In the original Greek text, this terminology referred to political overseers or leaders who had all the knowledge or wisdom of a city, village, or a town as they exercised oversight. He was referring to service that requires careful and wise oversight. However, Peter was not naïve. He recognized that there are special temptations associated with spiritual leadership, and so he mentions three sins and three antidotes through three contrasting phrases.

Not Under Compulsion

The first warning is to oversee the sheep not forcefully, but according to the will of God. Peter put it this way: "exercising oversight not under compulsion"—not because you're forced, not because someone's making you do it, but "voluntarily, according to the will of God." We shepherd people not because we have to but because we want to. Have you ever heard a pastor talk about their call to ministry by saying, "I was called into the ministry kicking and screaming. I didn't want to do it, but the Lord grabbed me by the collar and threw me into the pulpit?" When someone says that, I often want to reply, "I don't think it was God who did that."

Pastoral ministry is something you do willingly, something you were born to do, something you desire to do. Spurgeon declared that if you're a pastor who doesn't want to be in ministry, you're better off being a plumber. God doesn't call men into the ministry kicking and screaming. In 1 Timothy 3:1, Paul wrote, "If any man aspires to the office of overseer, it is a fine work he desires to do." Who wants to be under a pastor who says, "Well, I was going to make a million dollars, but God gave you to me to shepherd"? We must shepherd the flock willingly.

Not for Sordid Gain

Peter followed the charge of not serving under compulsion with a challenge concerning motivation. We are to pastor "not for sordid gain, but with eagerness" (1 Peter 5:2). The Authorized Version of the English Bible translates the phrase "sordid gain" as "filthy lucre"—in other words, for financial benefit or gain. First Timothy 3:3 informs us that an elder is to be "free from the love of money." Paul told Titus very clearly that elders and deacons are not to be fond of sordid gain (1:7).

It is important to observe that 1 Timothy provides instructions about remunerating elders who are worthy of double honor for their teaching and preaching. Paid pastors are part of God's economy. You don't muzzle the ox; you let him eat some of the fruit that he's helping to bear. Yet I get very disturbed when I hear of pastors and preachers who charge fees and require contracts when they are asked to speak at a conference or elsewhere. If you do pulpit supply or preach at conferences, does your decision to accept or decline the invitation depend on the size of the speaking fee? Do you consider the financial gain that you can appropriate because of ministerial relationships? You know what that's like—you're the pastor, you go to lunch, and you employ the fake reach for the check. You wait until the other person reaches, and then you reach. Pay for lunch, and don't be a freeloader! Peter's primary focus in his warning is for pastors to not profit from the ministry, because that adulterates the ministry.

Not Lording It Over People

Third, Peter wrote, "Nor yet as lording it over those allotted to your charge, but proving to be examples to the flock" (1 Peter 5:3). Note that Peter never says that the flock is yours. Rather, the charge is to be an *example* of what you teach, not an *exception* to what you teach. Peter implied that elders should not govern through threats, emotional intimidation, power, or the use of political force. Rather, you are to govern by example.

This, however, does not negate the authority of the elder. In verse 5, the congregation is commanded to "be subject to your elders." This implies that elders have genuine governing authority in the church, and that there are times when they have to give directions to the church. Wield this authority by example.

Jesus taught His disciples the same lesson in Mark 10:42: "Calling them to Himself, Jesus said to them, 'You know that those who are recognized as rulers of the Gentiles lord it over them; and their great men exercise authority over them.'" In contrast to this secular model, Jesus challenged His disciples as follows: "But it is not this way among you, but whoever wishes to become great among you shall be your servant; and whoever wishes to be first among you shall be slave of all. For even the Son of Man did not come to be served, but to serve, and to give His life a ransom for many" (verses 43-45). Spurgeon wrote,

> Whosoever will be chief among you, let him be your servant.
> Let us be willing to be doormats at our master's entrance hall.
> Let us not seek honor for ourselves, but put honor upon the
> weaker vessels with our care for them. In our Lord's church, let
> the poor, the feeble, the distressed have the place of honor and
> let us, who are strong bear their infirmities. He is highest who
> makes himself lowest. He is greatest, who makes himself less
> than the least.[4]

When Peter's audience read the words in 1 Peter 5:3-4, Ezekiel 34 must have been echoing in their minds. The prophet spoke on behalf of God in verse 1, saying, "The Word of the LORD came to me..." Upon hearing Ezekiel proclaim these words, his listeners may have been thinking, *Great, it's coming. We're going to hear of the judgment of the nations. We're going to hear more of the social injustices put in their place.* But here is what the spiritual leaders of Israel heard: "Son of man, prophesy against [drum roll] *the shepherds of Israel.*" The spiritual leaders must've thought, *Time out—we're on the same team!*

But Ezekiel continued, "Thus says the Lord GOD, 'Woe, shepherds of Israel who have been feeding themselves! Should not the shepherds feed the flock? You eat the fat and clothe yourselves with the wool, you slaughter the fat sheep without feeding the flock'" (Ezekiel 34:2–3). Ezekiel's words must have rocked the world of the kings, prophets, priests, synagogue leaders, and all those who were exercising any kind of spiritual oversight.

The shepherds were eating the fat and clothing themselves with the wool. They were only taking and not feeding. Ezekiel continued, "Those who are sickly you have not strengthened, the diseased you have not healed, the broken you have not bound up, the scattered you have not brought back, nor have you sought for the lost; but with force and with severity you have dominated them" (verse 4). Does that sound familiar? Domineering with severity and force. This passage had to be in Peter's mind. The fold of Israel was scattered because the people lacked a shepherd. In our modern context, I have heard that more people leave churches because they were uncared for than because they didn't like the preaching.

We continue reading in Ezekiel 34:5-6: "They were scattered for lack of a shepherd, and they became food for every beast of the field and were scattered. My flock wandered through all the mountains and on every high hill." They went to the hilltops because that was the only place sheep could find shelter from predators. Ezekiel continued,

> My flock was scattered over all the surface of the earth, and there was no one to search or seek for them. Therefore, you shepherds, hear the word of the LORD: "As I live," declares the Lord GOD, "surely because My flock has become a prey, My flock has even become food for all the beasts of the field for lack of a shepherd, and My shepherds did not search for My flock, but rather the shepherds fed themselves and did not feed My flock; therefore, you shepherds, hear the Word of the LORD: 'Thus says the Lord GOD, "Behold, I am against the shepherds"'" (verses 6-10).

Imagine for a moment God saying, "I am against the pastors." Then He says, "I will demand My sheep from them and make them cease from feeding sheep. So the shepherds will not feed themselves anymore, but I will deliver My flock from their mouth, so that they will not be food for them." God has to deliver His people from pastors because they are after the flock to exploit them for their own personal gain.

As pastors, we are not celebrities; we are servants. It's easier to stand high in the pulpit than to stoop low to wash feet. It's easier to preach at conferences than to visit widows and orphans. It's easier to lead seminars in public than to pray in solitude for our people. Ezekiel and Peter's emphasis is simply this: You pastor because you love God and you care for His flock.

How much time do you spend in the pulpit versus time with people?

Do you care? After you preach and you walk down from the pulpit, most of the people who want to talk to you are not coming to say, "You're great." They're coming to say, "Please notice me. Please care for me. You have said something that had spiritual attraction and divine authority, and I want to be shepherded." Your hearers typically don't come up to talk about your great exegesis; they want you to shepherd them. Preaching is an important part of the shepherd's crook. However, there are just a few verses about preaching, and there are a lot about pastoral care. How much time do you spend in the pulpit versus time with people?

All this comes back to what is written in Jeremiah 10:21: "The shepherds have become stupid and have not sought the LORD; therefore they have not prospered, and all their flock is scattered." The problem with some shepherds is that they have not sought the Lord. Care for your people and have them enjoy a better walk with Jesus because you're their *spiritual* leader.

Pastoral Ministry Is an Honorable Responsibility

The third sobering reality of pastoral ministry is that it is an honorable responsibility. First Peter 5:4 says, "When the Chief Shepherd appears, you will receive the unfading crown of glory." Peter stated the incentive for spiritual oversight—namely, the eternal reward to come. Ultimately a pastor's reward is not measured by financial remuneration or worldly glory, but by hearing Jesus say, "Well done, good and faithful servant, enter the joy of the Master" (see Matthew 25:23). One of the most beloved and familiar passages in the Bible is Psalm 23. When Peter uses the term, "Chief Shepherd," he echoed the psalm. Psalm 23 has been a comfort to many. It's so familiar that even nonbelievers know it. Read the psalm and pay attention to how it portrays the Chief Shepherd, who is our example.

In Psalm 23:1-2 we read, "The LORD is my shepherd, I shall not want. He makes me lie down in green pastures." Green pastures were rare in the ancient Near East. The land was mostly brown rubble and the shepherds would pick out patches of grass between rocks. The psalmist continued, "He leads me beside quiet waters. He restores my soul; He guides me in the paths of righteousness for His name's sake. Even though I walk through the valley of the shadow of death, I fear no evil, for You are with me" (verses 2-4). How many times do you get called to the hospital with a person who is about to die and what they want is for their pastor to pray and hold their hand as they take their final breath? "Your rod and Your staff, they comfort me. You prepare a table before me in the presence of my enemies; You have anointed my head with oil; my cup overflows. Surely goodness and lovingkindness will follow me all the days of my life, and I will dwell in the house of the LORD forever" (verses 4-6).

If you want to take a class on shepherdology, just read Psalm 23 and say, "I want to do that for my people." That's the nature of God's care. The analogy of God as a shepherd is obviously connected to the understanding that His people are the sheep, but it doesn't stop there. We read in Hebrews 13:20 that God "brought up from the dead the great Shepherd of the sheep through the blood of the eternal covenant, even Jesus our Lord." Jesus is our Chief Shepherd, and Peter wrote about this in 1 Peter 2:25: "You were continually straying like sheep, but now you have returned to the Shepherd and Guardian of your souls." God's shepherding is done primarily through proxy, through an approved stand-in for His name. In other words, God uses men to be shepherds for His sheep, and He still calls men to shepherd His flock today.

Remember as well what Jesus said in John 10:11: "I am the good shepherd; the good shepherd lays down His life for the sheep." And we see the contrast in John 10:12: "He who is a hired hand, and not a shepherd, who is not the owner of the sheep, sees the wolf coming, and leaves the sheep and flees, and the wolf snatches them and scatters them." The hired hand is in it for sordid gain and not for the care of the flock. This hired hand flees because he is a hired hand and is not concerned about the sheep.

Then Jesus said, "I am the good shepherd, and I know My own and My own know me, even as the Father knows Me and I know the Father; and I lay down My life for the sheep. I have other sheep, which are not of this fold; I must bring them also, and they will hear My voice; and they will become one flock with one shepherd" (John 10:13-16).

I read an article about shepherding that said shepherds in the Middle East usually have upwards of a 100 sheep that graze the same ground with three or four other shepherds. That means a pasture or hillside could have 300 to 400 sheep and several shepherds. And if one of the sheep happens to wander, the shepherd will call the sheep and it will respond to him because it knows his voice. This is what Jesus has in mind in John 10. Richard Baxter wrote to pastors, "We must feel toward our people as a Father toward his children. Yay, the most tender love of a mother must not surpass ours. We must even travail in birth until Christ is formed in them. They should see that we care for no outward thing."[5] The prophet Samuel said to the people of Israel, "Far be it from me that I should sin against the LORD by ceasing to pray for you" (1 Samuel 12:23). Interestingly, Samuel said that after he was out of a job.

The Goal of a Shepherd-Leader

All of what has been covered in this chapter is an introduction to Hebrews 13:17: "Obey your leaders and submit to them, for they keep watch over your souls as those who will give an account." Before you ask God to double the size of your church, make sure you're ready for double the amount of accountability. Before you ask God to fill the pews, make sure you're ready to pray for those who sit in them. Before you ask for a larger ministry, make sure you're asking for more time to be able to care for those people. Because the accountability and responsibility a shepherd has for the souls of God's flock is serious. When you think of the people as eternal souls with bodies, it changes the spectrum, dimensions, and depth of what you want to do. The goal of a shepherd-leader must be to shepherd his people so that they draw near to love and cherish the Chief Shepherd of their souls, Jesus Christ.

PRAYER

Father, I pray for spiritual leaders. Oh Lord, give us faithfulness. Give us an idea of our responsibilities before You make us responsible. Remind all of us that the flock we have is Your flock and they are Your sheep. Guard our hearts from filthy lucre, from prideful ambition, from domineering leadership, and from pastoring out of duty instead of delight. Help us take our cue from Jeremiah, who said that if we seek You, then and only then will we be shepherds after Your own heart. Oh Father, help us to extend Your pastoral care to Your flock through our humble efforts. In Jesus' name we pray, Amen.

GUARDING THE GOSPEL

"For am I now seeking the favor of men, or of God?"

GALATIANS 1:10

8

GUARDING THE GOSPEL

Steven J. Lawson
Shepherds' Conference 2009
Galatians 1:6-10

I am amazed that you are so quickly deserting Him who called you by the grace of Christ, for a different gospel; which is really not another; only there are some who are disturbing you and want to distort the gospel of Christ. But even if we, or an angel from heaven, should preach to you a gospel contrary to what we have preached to you, he is to be accursed! As we have said before, so I say again now, if any man is preaching to you a gospel contrary to what you received, he is to be accursed! For am I now seeking the favor of men, or of God? Or am I striving to please men? If I were still trying to please men, I would not be a bond-servant of Christ.

Every generation of believers in the church has had to fight for the purity and the exclusivity of the gospel of Jesus Christ. There is no exception. Beginning with Clement of Rome, Ignatius, and Justin Martyr, these men gave their own lives to preserve and to protect the purity of the gospel of Jesus Christ.

In the second century, Irenaeus fought Gnosticism, and Polycarp opposed the Roman proconsul at the cost of their lives. Cyprian fought apostasy in the third century and was sentenced to death. He removed his garments, knelt down, and only said, "Thanks be to God."[1]

In the fourth century Athanasius fought Arianism, which denied the deity of Christ and, thus, was a frontal attack against the gospel. Athanasius was unmoved, and he stood *contra mundum* against the world. He was willing to be one man standing for the gospel in the face of the entire world.

Augustine warred against Pelagius and his denial of the fall of the human race. John Wycliffe, John Huss, and Martin Luther attacked the perverted gospel of the Roman Catholic Church and its corrupt system of human works and merit. John Calvin fired volley after volley against Rome and its foul gospel, as well as against the Libertines, the Unitarians, and all other false sects.

In subsequent generations, Christian leaders continued to pay the ultimate price in order to preserve and protect the exclusivity of the gospel of Jesus Christ. John Rogers and the 284 Marian martyrs fought against the Roman Catholic Church over the nature of the Lord's Supper, which was in reality a fight over the nature of the purity of the gospel itself. Thomas Cranmer, Nicholas Ridley, and Hugh Latimer were burned at the stake at Oxford for the honor of the gospel. Latimer asserted to Ridley, "Be of good comfort, Master Ridley, and play the man: we shall this day light such a candle, by God's grace, in England, as I trust shall never be put out."[2] Six months earlier, Cranmer was physically removed from his pulpit and taken directly to the martyrs' stake and there he gave his life to uphold the standard of sound words.

Jonathan Edwards fought for the purity of the gospel against Arminianism and antinomianism. When the gospel was all but silenced in the Church of England, George Whitfield took to the open air and went out into the highways and the open fields. With a loud voice he proclaimed, "I have come here today to talk to you about your soul."[3] Asahel Nettleton fought for the gospel against Charles Finney, and Charles Spurgeon fought the Down-Grade Controversy over the message and the method of the gospel. So it goes in every generation. Every Christian leader worth his salt has fought for the gospel, and so must we.

This is exactly what Paul did in Galatians 1:6-10. He was waging war for the purity and the exclusivity of the gospel of Jesus Christ, and it is a hill worth dying on.

Fighting the Good Fight for the Gospel

The apostle Paul spent virtually his entire life fighting for the gospel. He opposed incipient Gnosticism among the Colossians. He waged war against secular philosophy, Jewish legalism, Eastern mysticism, and strict asceticism among the Galatians. He battled against those in Corinth who denied the resurrection of Christ. He even wrestled with fanaticism among the Thessalonians.

In Galatians, Paul contended against the Jewish legalism that had been brought into the church. This struggle would prove to be one of the most demanding conflicts of his life. In his defense of the gospel, Paul waged war against a group of false teachers known as the Judaizers. This group sought to mix law with grace, works with faith, and to put believers and unbelievers alike under the law of Moses. They claimed salvation must be earned by the law and that sanctification must be achieved by the works of the flesh. In response, the apostle Paul wrote this letter to the churches of Galatia, in which he heroically and valiantly fought the good fight for the gospel of Jesus Christ.

This epistle was Paul's most passionate letter. He dictated his other letters, but to write Galatians, he took his pen and wrote it himself. He wrote it in boxcar-size letters so large that anyone could clearly read what he was saying. He minced no words and breathed holy fire as he told all perverters of the gospel that they may go to hell before they deceive others. Along with rebuking the Judaizers, Paul was shocked that the Galatians had so quickly and so easily fallen for this false gospel. The time had come for Paul to address the issue directly and to have an adult conversation with the church.

Guarding the Gospel Today

We, as well, live in exactly such an hour. Not unlike the first century, the gospel of Jesus Christ is coming under attack again and again. There are many assaults upon the purity and the exclusivity of the gospel from cults, false religions, the Roman Catholic Church, the new perspective on

Paul, the non-lordship advocates, the social gospel proponents, the Universalists, and many others. There are many attacks upon the gospel, and it will fall upon each and every leader of Christ's church to act like men and to stand strong in the grace of God in defending the gospel. There is an ad in an athletic arena that reads, "We must protect this house." Shepherds, we must protect this gospel.

We need to heed Paul's words in these verses. We need to heed this warning that was sounded by him, and it must grip our hearts again. Let these words be as a trumpet in our ears. Let them be a drumbeat by which we march. Let them arrest our hearts and summon our souls.

We will categorize these verses into four main headings. *First*, Paul's amazement in verses 6 and 7. *Second*, Paul's adversaries at the end of verse 7. *Third*, Paul's anathemas in verses 8 and 9. *Fourth*, Paul's aim in verse 10.

Paul's Amazement

Paul expressed his astonishment over the Galatians in verse 6 as he wrote, "I am amazed." This word "amazed" is a strong word that means to be astounded, bewildered, and shocked. Paul was dumbfounded and perplexed at the news that he had received from the Galatians. He went on to say what he was amazed at: "That you are so quickly deserting Him" (1:6). He was shocked that the Galatians had abandoned the very gospel of Jesus Christ, which he had brought to them. The term "deserting" was used in the military to refer to a soldier who abandoned his position or post. It means to go AWOL. The Galatians had deserted their loyalty to God and their allegiance to the Lord Jesus Christ. The Greek verb is in the present tense, which reveals they were committing this action while Paul was writing the letter. At that very hour and at that very moment, they were in the process of deserting God Himself. Moreover, the Greek verb is in the middle voice, which implies that the Galatians were personally responsible for that act.

In deserting the gospel, the Galatians were deserting God. They were not merely deserting a system of theology, as important as that is, but the very God of that system. It is as if Paul was saying, "You are turning your backs on Almighty God. You are like military deserters. You are spiritual turncoats. You are defectors of the worse kind. I was just with you and delivered you the message, and now you are so quickly abandoning God." We can come to this conclusion because "God himself is the gospel." Therefore, to move away from the gospel is to move away from God. The gospel is God's gospel, and Romans 1:1 reminds us that the gospel is God's truth, God's power, God's message. And to abandon God's message is to abandon God Himself.

Every attribute of God is most beautifully put on display in the spectacle of the theater of the gospel of Jesus Christ. In Psalm 19:1 we read, "The heavens are telling of the glory of God." How much greater is the glory of God put on display in the message that tells us how to go to heaven? If God's glory is put on display in His creation, it is put on even greater display in His new creation through the gospel. Remember, it is in the gospel that we most clearly see the holiness of God. We see that God is transcended and majestic, high and lifted up, and is infinitely separated from defiled sinners.

The holiness of God comes shining forth brightly in the gospel of Jesus Christ, and begs for the solution to come from God. It is in the gospel that we see the wrath of God most vividly displayed. We see sin under judgment at the cross, and we see our sin judged by God in Christ. We behold Christ who became a curse for us, suffering in our place, receiving divine vengeance on our behalf. But it is also in the gospel that we see the righteousness of God. We see the righteousness of God that has been provided for us in the perfect obedience of Jesus Christ, in His sinless life, and in His substitutionary death. It is in the gospel that we see the grace of God providing righteousness for sinners.

All of the lines of theology proper intersect in the gospel of Jesus Christ, and all of the attributes of God intersect in the person and work of Christ, who is the gospel for us.

It is in the gospel that we see the immutability of God, that there is but one unchanging way of salvation from beginning to end. It is in the gospel that we behold the power of God that is able to save the chief of sinners and that is able to transform and sanctify the vilest of rebels. It is in the gospel that we see the truth of God and the reality of His saving enterprise made known to us. It is in the gospel that we see the sovereignty of God, saving all of His elect, all those chosen by the Father and entrusted to Christ. All of the lines of theology proper intersect in the gospel of Jesus Christ, and all of the attributes of God intersect in the person and work of Christ, who is the gospel for us. To defect from the gospel is to defect from God Himself.

In verse 6, Paul continued, "I am amazed that you are so quickly deserting Him who called you by the grace of Christ." The Galatians deserted God after He had provided for them salvation through sovereign, irresistible, and effectual grace. This grace had called them, overpowered their resistance to God, and drawn them to Himself to be trophies of His grace.

This God who had called them by His pure, sheer, and unadulterated grace was rejected when they turned to a "different gospel."

There are only two kinds of gospels. There is the true gospel, and there is the false gospel. There is the gospel that saves, and a false gospel that condemns. Paul was claiming that the Galatians had deserted the gospel of divine accomplishment for a gospel of human achievement. This different gospel, or *heteron* gospel, denotes another of a totally different kind. A modern-day comparison is the idiom that we are comparing apples to oranges. This message that had crept into Galatia was a totally different message that was a nonsaving and nonsanctifying gospel of legalism. It was a counterfeit gospel, a sham salvation, and a rip-off religion. As a result, Paul pleaded with them to turn back to the true gospel.

At the beginning of verse 7, Paul wrote concerning this different gospel that it "is really not another"—which is to say there is only one true gospel. There is only one true way of salvation, and any other message is soul-damning. There is only one way of salvation because Jesus said, "I am the way, and the truth, and the life; no one comes to the Father but through Me" (John 14:6). Peter preached, "There is salvation in no one else; for there is no other name under heaven that has been given among men by which we must be saved" (Acts 4:12). Paul wrote, "There is one God, and one mediator also between God and men, the man Christ Jesus"

(1 Timothy 2:5). To desert this gospel is to be removed from the only way of salvation.

Jesus is the only way of salvation because no one else has been born of a virgin, lived a sinless and perfect life, given His perfect righteousness, died in the sinner's place, bore the sins of man, suffered the wrath of God, reconciled sinners to an infinitely holy God, redeemed us out of our slavery to sin and Satan, raised for our justification, and is seated at the right hand of God the Father. No one else has ever done all this—not Buddha, Allah, Mary, the pope, some Unitarian being, Joseph Smith, Mary Baker Eddy, and certainly not me on my own behalf. No one else but Jesus Christ sent from God.

Paul was amazed that the Galatians had deserted this one true saving gospel and so should we be astonished whenever we see such desertion in our own day. We should be bewildered when we see evangelicals want to sign something like an ECT (Evangelicals and Catholics Together) document and pretend that there is no difference between Rome and the gospel of Jesus Christ.

We should be astonished when we see certain so-called Christian leaders go on television and punt away the gospel. Larry King interviewed a known pastor and started the conversation with the following words: "We've had ministers on our program who said you either believe in Christ or you don't. If you believe in Christ you're going to heaven. If you don't, no matter what you've done in your life, you aren't." The response from his guest, a prominent so-called Christian leader, was, "Yeah, I don't know. I believe you have to know Christ, but I think that if you know Christ, if you're a believer in God, that you're going to have some good works. I think it's a cop out to say, 'I'm a Christian, but I don't ever do anything.'"[4]

King responded, "What if you're Jewish? What if you're a Muslim and you don't accept Christ at all?"[5] The answer, "You know, I'm very careful about saying who would and who wouldn't go to heaven. I don't know." King responded, "If you believe you have to believe in Christ, they're [Jews and Muslims] wrong, aren't they?" His guest responded: "I don't know if I'd believe they're wrong. I spent a lot of time in India with my father. I don't know about all their religion, but I know they love God. I don't know. I've seen their sincerity."

No, they do not love God; they hate God. Give us leaders who know the truth, who will declare the truth, who will stand with Athanasius, Polycarp, Calvin, Luther, Whitfield, and Edwards, and who will declare from the housetops that the gospel is the only power of God unto salvation. Paul was amazed that some were willing to desert the gospel, and so should we be astonished and bewildered at this hour of history.

Paul's Adversaries

Second, in Galatians 1:7, we see Paul's adversaries. The problem of the false gospel was with the opponents, who were corrupting and disturbing the believers. We observe in the middle of verse 7 Paul mentioning the false teachers for the first time, though not by name: "Only there are *some…*" (emphasis mine). Draw a circle around the word "some." These *some* are the Judaizers who were trying to bring their legalism into the church and put the people under the law; as a result, they are "disturbing you." *To disturb* is the Greek word *tarassontes,* and it means to trouble, to agitate, or to shake up. These false teachers had come into the vacuum during Paul's absence and they had filled it up with their corrupt gospel.

The false teachers were shaking up the allegiance of the believers to God Himself. In so doing, they were disturbing and troubling the church. For if you take away the gospel, you have taken away everything. "Only there are some who are disturbing you and want to distort the gospel of Christ" (verse 7). The word "distort" means to transform something into the very opposite of what it is. The Judaizers were changing the true gospel and morphing it into a false gospel. They were tampering with the message, deluding its purity, and distorting its essence. These Judaizers were teaching Christ, grace, and faith, but these alone were inadequate to save and to sanctify. They were saying human works are also necessary for salvation and religious effort is required for acceptance with God. However, Paul wrote in 2:21, "If righteousness comes through the Law, then Christ died needlessly." If we can achieve our own salvation apart from the sufficiency of the cross, then Calvary is the blunder of the ages.

There are many adversaries of the gospel today. They acknowledge a place for the cross, they speak of grace, they pontificate about faith, but simultaneously they claim that faith is not enough to be right with God.

They claim that salvation is by faith and good works, faith and water baptism, faith and church membership, faith and speaking in tongues, faith and Hail Marys, faith and the mass, faith and the last rites, faith and the treasury of merit, faith and buying indulgences. They claim that all of these are necessary for salvation, and as a result they damn the souls of men.

Of course, there are adversaries to the gospel of a theological kind. They deny the Trinity, the absolute deity of Jesus Christ, the lordship of Christ, the virgin birth, the sinless life of Jesus, substitutionary death, the bodily resurrection of Jesus, and Jesus' second coming. Others reject the exclusivity of salvation in Christ alone and say, "Jesus is only one of many roads that lead to the mountaintop where God is." But if Jesus is not the only way to heaven, then He is none of the ways to heaven, for Jesus claimed to be the only way of salvation, and a liar cannot be our Savior. J.C. Ryle wrote that if we truly believe that Christ is the only way of salvation, then it will mark our preaching and empower our proclamation. As ministers, we will speak of Christ and our sermons will be filled with Christ because He is the only way of salvation.[6]

The true gospel is centered on God's salvation through His Son, the Lord Jesus Christ. Jesus, who is fully God and fully man, sacrificed Himself on the cross for our sins. On the cross, He became sin for us, bore our sins, died in our place, and suffered under the wrath of God so that sinners may be rescued from this present evil age. This whole world is a planet under judgment. We read in Romans 1:18, "The wrath of God is revealed from heaven against all ungodliness and unrighteousness of men who suppress the truth in unrighteousness." Right now, this very hour, we are a planet under judgment from a holy God. There is only one way of rescue, and it is to come to the cross of the Lord Jesus Christ and by faith believe upon Him. This is the gospel.

Paul affirmed this truth in Galatians 2:16: "A man is not justified by the works of the Law but through faith in Christ Jesus." Justification is the forensic declaration of the holy judge. Justification is God's declaration of the righteousness of Christ being imputed to sinners who believe upon Jesus. This declaration and imputation is by grace alone, through faith alone, in Christ alone. Luther said, "This is the chief article from which all other doctrines have flowed. It alone begets, nourishes, builds, preserves, and defends the church of God. Without the church of God, it cannot exist for one hour."[7] Luther went on to say that the doctrine of justification is the chief matter upon which the church stands or falls.[8] This was the master truth that those who had come into Galatia had corrupted, perverted, and tainted. It was the truth of justification that Paul defended as he spoke out against the false teachers.

Paul's Anathemas

We have beheld Paul's amazement and adversaries, and third we see Paul's anathemas. These Judaizers sought to undermine Paul's teaching of the gospel, and in Galatians 1:8 Paul put forward an extreme hypothetical situation in order to make his point. He began with a radical statement when he said, "Even if we…" Even if Paul, Barnabas, Timothy, Luke, or "an angel from heaven"—Michael the archangel; Gabriel, one of the chief angels or one of the ruling angels or guardian angels; one of the seraphim, cherubim, or any of the elect angels—"should preach to you a gospel contrary to what we have preached to you, he is to be accursed!"

If any of these persons should preach a gospel that was contrary to salvation by grace through faith in Christ, that individual was to be "accursed" (Greek, *anathema*). That is a potent word, for it means to be devoted to destruction or to be consigned to the flames of eternal hell below. In other words, it means to be damned to hell. To put it bluntly, Paul was saying, "They should go to hell before they take anyone else with them into the pit below." This is the man who can be worked up over that which works up the heart of God.

Martin Luther provided a colorful commentary on this passage when he wrote, "Paul is breathing fire. His zeal is so fervent that he almost begins to curse the angels themselves."[9] There was no room for neutrality, no room for indifference, no room for passivity, for this was a time for Paul to defend the gospel. James Montgomery Boice wrote, "How can it be otherwise? If the gospel Paul preaches is true, then the glory of Jesus Christ and the salvation of men are at stake. If men can be saved by works, then Christ has died in vain. The cross is emptied of power. If men are taught a false gospel, they are being led from the one thing that can save them…to destruction."[10] How true are these words spoken by Boice, because those who corrupt the one true saving gospel contribute to the damnation of lost souls.

Paul reloaded in verse 9 and dogmatically asserted that his message was consistent to what the Galatians had heard before. He wrote, "As we have said before..." Paul referred to the time he was in Galatia amidst the churches. He was emphatic in underscoring that he had not altered his message, which he received not from men but from Christ. He said, "If any man"—whether an apostle, an angel, or a self-appointed religious leader—"is preaching" (notice the present tense) "to you a gospel contrary to what you received, he is to be accursed!" Paul repeated this shocking statement to emphasize the severity of the judgment that awaits the false prophet. The hottest place in hell is reserved for those false teachers who distort the gospel of Christ and drag others down into the pit below.

I would remind us that Paul put these words on the front porch of this book. This is where Paul, in his other epistles, usually expressed his thanksgiving to God for the churches. Paul would normally write early in his letter, "Oh, how I thank God for you. You are in my every thought. You give me so much joy." Yet there is none of that in the epistle to the Galatians. Instead of being thankful, the apostle was rightly filled with holy zeal because the glory of God and of Christ had been contaminated with this false message. Paul was worked up about this because the only saving gospel and sanctifying message was at stake.

In doing this, Paul was following in the steps of his Master. Jesus Himself warned against false religious leaders who would pervert the true way of salvation. Jesus said, "Enter through the narrow gate; for the gate is wide and the way is broad that leads to destruction, and there are many who enter through it. For the gate is small and the way is narrow that leads to life, and there are few who find it" (Matthew 7:13-14). Jesus concluded by saying, "Beware of the false prophets, who come to you in sheep's clothing, but inwardly are ravenous wolves" (7:15). Paul's anathemas were rightly spoken. This was no time for dialogue. This was the time for declaration.

Paul's Aim

Fourth, we see Paul's aim, which should be the aim of every single leader who shepherds God's flock. This is what every preacher and every

Christian must wrestle with: "Am I now seeking the favor of men, or of God?" (Galatians 1:10). There are no other categories and no other options. Either we live our life to receive the approbation of God in heaven, or we play to the applause of the crowd. If Paul was seeking the favor of men, he would have toned down his rhetoric. But Paul was not courting the popularity of the world. He was not even courting the popularity of the church and the churches to whom this book was written. Paul was writing that he might receive his "Amens" out of heaven. Paul was seeking the approbation of God by writing what God had said. This harsh language was hardly calculated to win the approval of men, for men-pleasers simply do not hurl anathemas against those who proclaim false gospels. Paul was not concerned about that because he sought to please God.

Ministry is simple—we ultimately must seek the favor and the approval of the Almighty God.

Who Will You Please?

Here is that with which you and I must come to grips. If we seek to please God, it does not matter whom we displease. If we displease God, it does not matter whom we please. Ministry is simple—we ultimately must seek the favor and the approval of the Almighty God. Paul wrote, "If I were still trying to please men, I would not be a bond-servant of Christ" (Galatians 1:10). In the ultimate sense, pleasing men and pleasing God are mutually exclusive, not inclusive. Either you seek to please men, and if so you will displease God; or if you seek to please God, then you are willing to displease men. Even our Lord said in Matthew 6:24, "No one can serve two masters; for either he will hate the one and love the other, or he will be devoted to one and despise the other." Jesus understood we can have only one master and as slaves of Christ, we report to Him and seek His approval.

Paul wrote in 1 Thessalonians 2:4, "Just as we have been approved by God to be entrusted with the gospel, so we speak, not as pleasing men, but

God who examines our hearts." Paul realized that he was chosen by God, called by God, set apart by God, saved by God, redeemed by God, commissioned by God, enlightened by God, instructed by God, appointed by God, empowered by God, and directed by God. Why on earth would he suddenly seek to please men?

Paul knew that in the last day, it will be God before whom we stand. We will be judged, not by men or angels, but by God, and we will either be rewarded or passed over. Therefore, it is God whom we must please, and there is only one message that pleases God: the true gospel of Jesus Christ, which is salvation by grace alone, through faith alone, in Christ alone.

An Example to Follow

One of the most courageous men to walk this earth with the gospel was John Knox. I had the privilege, a couple of years ago, to stand with Dr. MacArthur where Knox is buried, and to step in Knox's pulpit. John Knox, a Roman Catholic priest in Scotland, was converted by the power of the gospel and became a bodyguard of George Wishart. Wishart was martyred and his ministry was passed on to Knox. He began to preach in St. Andrew's castle and was soon captured and taken aboard a French ship. He served in the hull of that ship for the next 19 months as a captive of war. When he was released, he came back to Scotland to preach the gospel.

When Bloody Mary took the throne, Knox fled Scotland and went to Geneva to pastor an English-speaking congregation. He even played a role in the production of the Geneva Bible. However, once Bloody Mary was removed from the throne, Knox returned to Scotland. Mary, Queen of Scots, took on the throne, and on her very first Sunday as queen of Scotland, she went into the solitude of her own chapel, where she received a private mass. This news reached the ears of John Knox, and on the very next Sunday, at St. Giles Church in Edinburgh, Scotland, he ascended into to the pulpit and called out the queen. He declared from the pulpit, "One mass is more fearful to me than if 10,000 armed enemies were landed in any part of this realm." Knox said, "I have learned plainly and boldly to call wickedness by its own terms. I call a fig, a fig and a spade, a spade."[11]

When word reached Mary, Queen of Scots, she was infuriated. She summoned Knox to appear before her in order to give an account of his declaration. Knox came in, and the queen took the offensive. She launched with three indictments and charges to be brought against John Knox, and yet the charges deflected off of him like water on a duck's back. Knox did not mince words when he declared to her the idolatry of the mass, asserting that the mass could have no place in Scotland, for it would invite the judgment of God upon the nation. Knox was unrelenting in preaching to her the one true pure saving gospel of grace in the Lord Jesus Christ. Consequently, she was reduced to a puddle of tears. Knox recorded that she began to howl like a wounded animal. The cause of the Reformation in Scotland turned as a result of a series of six encounters between the thundering Scot, John Knox, and Mary, Queen of Scots.

When Knox died on December 24, 1572 in Edinburgh, the region of Scotland spoke these long-remembered words over Knox's grave: "Here lies a man who in his life never feared the face of man."[12] Perhaps Knox is best summarized by the closing words of the Scots Confession that he penned in 1560 upon his return to Scotland: "Arise, O Lord and let thine enemies be confounded. Let them flee from thy presence, that hate thy godly name. Give thy servants strength to speak thy word with boldness, and let all nations cleave to the true knowledge of thee."[13]

Where are such leaders today? As someone once observed, the problem with preachers today is no one wants to kill them anymore. Where are those who will say with Paul, "If any man is preaching to you a gospel contrary to what you received, he is to be accursed!" (Galatians 1:9)? I hope there are such men reading these words even now.

PRAYER

Rise up, O men of God, have done with lesser things.
Give heart and mind and soul and strength to serve the
King of kings. Let us preach the gospel, teach the gospel,
live the gospel, explain the gospel, and expand the gospel,
and let the chips fall where they may. Let us please God.
Let us not become men-pleasers.

No Little People,
No Little Sermons

"Jesus answered, 'It was neither that this man sinned,
nor his parents; but it was so that the works of God
might be displayed in him.'"

LUKE 9:3

9

NO LITTLE PEOPLE,
NO LITTLE SERMONS

Albert Mohler Jr.
Shepherds' Conference 2010
John 9:1-42

"We proclaim Him, admonishing every man and teaching every man with all wisdom, so that we may present every man complete in Christ" (Colossians 1:28). That is what the preacher of the Word gets to do. That is what the preacher of the Word is assigned to do. That is what the preacher of the Word had better do. God is calling men to preach His Word by supernaturally equipping them to accomplish this task. Yet not everyone heeds this mandate.

I recently had the opportunity to preach at a convention. As I was walking into the hotel ballroom to preach, I noticed strobe lights and all kinds of special effects, but I did not see a pulpit. They said, "Don't worry, it's electronic." I said, "My worry is it's invisible." They responded, "Don't worry, it will appear when you get ready to preach," and I was forced to practice faith. Then when it was time to preach, behold the floor opened and pipes appeared. On top of thin purple pipes there sat a wooden plate. On top of the wooden plate there stood a microphone, and I assumed that I was to stand behind the pipes and the plate.

As I got up behind the pipes and the plate—improvised as a pulpit—I thought, *I'm not sure exactly what this symbolizes. It could symbolize the cross-cultural power of the pulpit, or it could symbolize the disappearance of the pulpit because it is so conveniently put away.* In far too many churches there is an absence of the pulpit because there is an absence of preaching. The disappearance of the pulpit is the hallmark of the age. Have you noticed the unbearable lightness of so much of what is called preaching? Have you noticed the unbearable lightness of so many sermons being "small"? "Big" sermons are important, but big does not always equate to long. In the New Testament, some brief sermons have huge implications. Today, however, many long sermons actually contain small amounts of truth.

Bringing Weight to Our Sermons

As pastors, our efforts will be weighed in the balances, and we will find out how "big" the ministry was. We will stand before our Maker, the judge of all, and find out how large our sermons were. We worship an infinite God and proclaim an infinite gospel. The New Testament describes the eternal weight of glory that is at stake. Francis Schaeffer wrote a book entitled *No Little People, No Little Places.* I hope if nothing else, that title encourages you. There are no little people, no little places, and the weight of a ministry is not determined by its size. Since there are no little people, there had better be no little sermons. Little sermons will not do.

As leaders, we need the reminder that people are important. Therefore, we must recognize the need to bring weight to our sermons.

As a leader of God's flock, you cannot overestimate the power of His Word. This is affirmed in the ninth chapter of the Gospel of John with the account of a man born blind who is healed. We see here a fascinating set of discussions, interrogations, and the revelation of the glory of God. This passage contains much irony—blindness, light, sight, eyes that will not see, eyes that are opened to see, and eyes thrown out from the temple because they now see. We are told that as Jesus passed by he saw a man blind from birth. The disciples, however, did not see a man. They saw a question. In seeing the man, Jesus reaffirmed that there are no little people. As leaders, we need the reminder that people are important. Therefore, we must recognize the need to bring weight to our sermons.

Seeing the Question vs. Seeing the Man

Jesus' disciples looked at the man and asked, "Rabbi, who sinned, this man or his parents, that he would be born blind?" (John 9:2). This question is not foolish. As a matter of fact, in the teaching context of Jesus, that question would come to mind to anyone who is theologically inquisitive. There must be a reason or rationale for the blindness. Surely, we can identify a causative agent. A sin or an entire complex of sin must explain this.

Now, the problem is more complicated than it may appear. The direct linkage between sin and consequence may be apparent in some cases. For example, someone might have become blind due to traceable sin like fetal alcohol syndrome or another clear causative explanation. However, there is no direct explanation here that makes any sense to the disciples other than sin. Like the friends of Job, they immediately followed the conventional theological thinking of the time and imagined this misfortune was caused by someone's sin. Because the man was born blind, they suggested it could be the parents' fault. Perhaps some other explanation existed. So the disciples asked, "Rabbi, who sinned, this man or his parents, that he would be born blind?"

Theologically, the answer is sin because we live in a Genesis 3 world. Every disaster found in Scripture points to the fall and explains, in nonnegotiable terms, that every single thing that goes wrong—all sin, evil, and even what we might define as natural or moral evil—is traceable directly to the fall. Earthquakes, tsunamis, mosquitoes, and tapeworms are all because of Genesis 3. In one sense, sin is the right answer. It is not the sufficient answer, however, to the disciples' question. And Jesus responded in a way that did not fit the conventional wisdom of their theology.

The Errors of Assigning Suffering

The disciples asked this question presumptuously. John Calvin suggested three reasons why we err in assigning a reason for suffering and

tying it to specific sin.[1] *First*, we err because we see sin and its consequences far more easily in others than we do in ourselves. The *second* reason is what he called immoderate severity. By that he meant we are poor
judges of quantifiable suffering. How would we presume to have some
adequate insight to measure why the consequence of this sin might be this
suffering? Calvin said we have no meter that can guide us with any kind
of accuracy there. It's sheer presumptuousness and arrogance on the part
of the creature to try to determine this.[2] *Third*, Calvin wrote that there is
now no condemnation for those who are in Christ Jesus. Yet, those who
are Christ's still suffer.[3] That ought to warn us against presumptuousness.
The disciples saw an understandable question, but Jesus saw a man and
healed him. However, before He healed him, He made a comment to His
disciples that was both a response and a retort. He said, "It was neither
that this man sinned, nor his parents; but it was so that the works of God
might be displayed in him" (verse 3).

Jesus affirmed that the focus was not on whether this man or his parents sinned. The causative agent here has a very different agenda, plan, and
purpose in mind. This man was born blind so that the works of God might
be displayed in him. Jesus went on to say, "We must work the works of
Him who sent Me as long as it is day; night is coming when no one can
work. While I am in the world, I am the Light of the world" (verses 4-5).
Every human, every believer in the Lord Jesus Christ, and especially every
preacher needs to hear that word. We must be aware of this command to
work the works of Him who called us while it is day, since night is coming,
when no man can work. There is a set time for our ministry. We and our
ministries are finite. With every tick of the clock, turn of the calendar, and
breath we take, we move closer to our death than to our birth. We progress closer to that time when no man can work. Thus, we must do what
Jesus commands. We must work the works of Him who sent us while it is
day. Night is coming, when no man can work.

Then Jesus began to teach about His identity, similar to what He had
told us already in John 8. There He said, "I am the Light of the world;
he who follows Me will not walk in the darkness, but will have the Light
of life" (John 8:12). In response, the Pharisees confronted Him and said,

"You are testifying about Yourself; Your testimony is not true" (verse 13). Jesus answered, "Even if I testify about Myself, My testimony is true, for I know where I came from and where I am going; but you do not know where I come from or where I am going" (verse 14). Jesus revealed Himself as the light of the world, but the Pharisees rebuked and rejected Him.

When Jesus spoke to His own disciples, He repeated the same phrase: "I am the Light of the world" (John 9:5). As the light of the world, Jesus healed the blind man so that the works of God would be displayed in him. Notice how Jesus healed this man. He spat on the ground, made clay out of the spittle, applied the clay to the man's eyes, and said to him: "Go, wash in the pool of Siloam" (verse 7). The man did exactly what he was told to do, but the healing was passive. He merely received what the Lord had done for him. Jesus' actions are powerfully symbolic as we are all made out of clay—the dust of the ground.

We continue in the narrative and read the stunning words of John 9:7: "So he went away and washed, and came back seeing." He went away a blind man, feeling his way to the pool of Siloam, and he came back seeing. How could anyone preach a little sermon about that? Blindness became sight. Darkness became light. The disciples saw a question, but Jesus saw a man. Jesus made clear to His disciples that this man's blindness was not an occasion for them to ask a theological question. Instead, it was an occasion for the incarnate Son of God, the light of the world, to spit on the very ground that He had made, take the spittle, put it on the man's eyes, and send him to wash. The blind man went, washed, and came back seeing. You cannot preach a little sermon about that, and that's not even the end of the text. After darkness and blindness had become light and sight, the questioners came to figure out what this meant.

The Neighbors See a Question

Now that the man was no longer blind, his neighbors saw him as a question. The narrator wrote, "Therefore the neighbors, and those who previously saw him as a beggar, were saying, 'Is not this the one who used to sit and beg?'" (John 9:8). The neighbors had not failed to notice him since by definition, in the New Testament era, a blind man was a beggar.

They knew him and had identified him. Yet they ignored him, felt superior to him, and may have even felt pity upon him.

Note what doesn't happen in this passage: No one celebrated that this blind man could now see. His neighbors did not. His parents did not. The Pharisees surely did not. Notice the question the neighbors posed: "Is this not the one who used to sit and beg?" They knew him as the blind man who sat and begged, but now he sees. We continue reading: "Others were saying, 'This is he,' still others were saying, 'No, but he is like him.' He kept saying, 'I am the one'" (verse 9). Notice the confusion here. Others were saying, "No, but he is like him." In other words, if you get used to ignoring people, they all look alike. But he kept saying, "I am the one. I was blind, but now I see. You were the people who saw me when I was blind, when I could not see. Now I see, and you do not see me."

The people asked him other questions. Evidently they came to an adequate confidence that this was the blind beggar: "So they were saying to him, 'How then were your eyes opened?'" (verse 10). He explained, "The man who is called Jesus made clay, and anointed my eyes, and said to me, 'Go to Siloam and wash'; so I went away and washed, and I received sight" (verse 11). The answer was accurate and pristine. Then, "they said to him, 'Where is He?' He said, 'I do not know'" (verse 12). His response was legitimate. The man had done what Jesus had told him to do. When he came back, he knew who had healed him, but he did not know where Jesus was.

The next question that arose was a theological one: Was the man clean or unclean? We are not able to exhaustively trace the biblical system of determining what was clean or unclean. What would have determined if this man was to be recognized as clean was the adjudication of the nature of this miracle. The miracle was unprecedented in terms of their experience and demanded some kind of explanation. As a result, the people brought the healed man to the experts—Theologians "R" Us—the Pharisees. The narrator wrote, "They brought to the Pharisees the man who was formerly blind" (verse 13). Now matters get complicated because it was the Sabbath when Jesus made the clay and opened the man's eyes. Jesus had a pattern of healing people on the Sabbath: the man at the Pool of Bethesda, the man with the withered hand, and now this man. If there was anything the Pharisees could not stand, it was a miracle on the Sabbath.

The Pharisees were confronted with a man who was formerly blind and was healed on the Sabbath: "Now it was a Sabbath on the day when Jesus made the clay and opened his eyes. Then the Pharisees also were asking him again how he received his sight. And he said to them, 'He applied clay to my eyes, and I washed, and I see'" (verses 14-15). It was a three-stage operation: clay, wash, see. "Therefore some of the Pharisees were saying, 'This man is not from God, because He does not keep the Sabbath.' But others were saying, 'How can a man who is a sinner perform such signs?' And there was a division among them" (John 9:16). One of the interesting ironies embedded in this account is that the formerly blind man had not identified Jesus as the one who had healed him. Nonetheless, the Pharisees already know who it was.

A division formed among the Pharisees over whether or not a man who was a sinner could perform such signs. They returned to the blind man and said to him, "What do you say about Him, since He opened your eyes?" (verse 17). Now that's a fascinating question. John, inspired by the Holy Spirit, gave us the most incredible weight of irony here. The Pharisees, the ones who couldn't see, asked the question, "What do you say about it?" Now remember, the man was brought to them because they were the experts, and yet they were saying to him, "Provide input." He did, and said, "He is a prophet" (verse 17).

Here was a formerly blind man who had been ignored by virtually everyone. Now they were asking him for answers. He had become the theologian. He had a category for Jesus: prophet. This once-blind man didn't know everything, but he knew that no sinner could have healed him.

In verse 18 we read, "The Jews then did not believe it of him, that he had been blind and had received sight, until they called the parents of the very one who had received his sight." When the Pharisees didn't receive the answer that they wanted, they assumed that he was not who he said he was. So the people called in the man's parents and brought them to the Pharisees. This would have been a terrifying experience for them because for them to give the wrong answer might cause them to be cast out from the synagogue. The parents were confronted with their own son, and they must have had many of the same questions as the Pharisees: Why was he blind? How did this happen? Now their son, who was blind and a beggar, sees. Having been ignored, he's now the center of attention, and so are the parents. The Pharisees asked, "Is this your son, who you say was born blind?" (verse 19). We must remember that blindness was considered a blight and a curse. The Pharisees continued, "Then how does he now see?"

The parents responded, "We know that this is our son, and that he was born blind; but how he now sees, we do not know; or who opened his eyes, we do not know" (verses 20-21). They knew this was their son, and they knew he was born blind. But as to how he now sees, "We do not know." Or who opened his eyes? "We do not know." Then, in effect, they throw their own son under the bus: "Ask him; he is of age, he will speak for himself" (verse 21). We are told that his parents said this because "they were afraid of the Jews; for the Jews had already agreed that if anyone confessed Him to be Christ, he was to be put out of the synagogue" (verse 22).

The scene shifted again, and the man was brought back for a second interrogation: "So a second time they called the man who had been blind, and said to him, 'Give glory to God; we know that this man is a sinner'" (verse 24). This statement was a warning to be careful. Then we find out just how much of a theologian this fellow is in verse 25: "He then answered, 'Whether He is a sinner, I do not know; one thing I do know, that though I was blind, now I see.'" His primary concern was not a matter of theological nicety and attempting to resolve the Pharisees' dilemma. He would not be entrapped by their corrupted way of thinking. Instead, his response was, "You put that question aside, here's what I know: I was blind—ask my parents—and now I see."

That is the paradigmatic Christian testimony. John 9 is not just an account about a man who was born blind who now sees. This entire chapter is about the display of the glory of God through the blind receiving sight. John weaved the narrative together to show that those who are spiritually blind are unable to see spiritual realities.

The Pharisees then asked the man, "What did He do to you? How did He open your eyes?" (verse 26). They had already asked that question, and it had already been answered. But he answered yet again, "I told you already and you did not listen; why do you want to hear it again? You do not want to become His disciples too, do you?" (verse 27). Here's what we discover about this man: Not only was he a theologian, but he was also incredibly perceptive and brave. He had the courage to ask the Pharisees, "You do not want to become His disciples too, do you?"

The Man Sees Jesus as He Is

The disciples saw a question, Jesus saw a man, and the man saw Jesus as He was. The man mockingly asked the Pharisees, "Is that what's going on here? Do you want to become his disciples?" How did they respond? "They reviled him and said, 'You are His disciple, but we are disciples of Moses'" (John 9:28). These were the same folks who said, "We are the children of Abraham" (see John 8:33). Jesus responded, "No, you're not, because before Abraham was, I was. Abraham knew Me. You're no sons of Abraham."

Now they say to this man, "We are disciples of Moses." The Pharisees think they know something when they say, "We know that God has spoken to Moses, but as for this man, we do not know where He is from" (John 9:29). Just imagine this man's experience. He was blind and now he could see. And he has discovered that the world wasn't as he thought it was. The world was not made up of sighted people. It was made up of blind people! Up till now he had assumed that he was blind and everyone else had sight. Now he has come to understand that blind people have surrounded him all his life.

The man then said, "Here is an amazing thing, that you do not know where He is from, and yet he opened my eyes. We know that God does not hear sinners; but if anyone is God-fearing and does His will, He hears him" (verses 30-31). How many times must the man have prayed to receive sight during all those years of sitting there begging? He never received sight, and then one day came Jesus. Now he could see. He continued, "Since the beginning of time it has never been heard that anyone opened the eyes of a person born blind. If this man were not from God, He could do nothing" (verses 32-33). This layman told the panel of theologians—the experts in the law—that if this man was not from God, He could do nothing.

Their response was an affirmation of only one thing: "They answered

him, 'You were born entirely in sins, and are you teaching us?'" (verse 34).
They only affirmed their faulty theological position. They hadn't learned
a thing and still thought God's judgment was upon the man. What do
you do when you have a theological problem you can't resolve? The only
answer is that a sovereign God has acted. If you're the Pharisees, however,
you "put him out" (verse 34). And that's what they did.

"Jesus heard that [the Pharisees] had put the man out, and finding
him, He said, 'Do you believe in the Son of Man?'" (John 9:35). This
man had been asked many questions. He had answered honestly and
directly with amazing courage and remarkable candor. He had also
answered with the knowledge that could come only to a man who had
been touched by the Savior. Now the very One who gave him sight asked
him a question. The man answered, "Who is He, Lord, that I may believe in
Him?" (verse 36). He was ready to believe anything that this Man told him.

Notice how Jesus answered: "You have both seen Him, and He is the
one who is talking with you" (verse 37). The man responded with a simple profession of faith: "Lord, I believe" (verse 38). Salvation had come not
only to his eyes, but also to his soul. He did not only see, but he came to
believe. He not only professed with his lips, but he also worshiped Jesus.
Then Jesus clarified all that had happened as only He can: "For judgment
I came into this world, so that those who do not see may see, and that
those who see may become blind" (John 9:39). Jesus came to confirm the
world's blindness. Earlier, John taught us that Jesus came to His own, and
His own received Him not (1:11).

When Some Remain Blind

In stark contrast to the narrative, the Pharisees then asked a pathetic
question: "We are not blind too, are we?" (John 9:40). If you have to ask
whether you are blind, you just might be blind. Jesus answered them with
a word of severe judgment: "If you were blind, you would have no sin; but
since you say, 'We see,' your sin remains" (verse 41). Their problem was not
with physical blindness, but with a blindness of a completely different category. They were willfully, spiritually, and theologically blind.

They could not see because they would not see. The deadly reality of
blindness is evident in this exchange between Jesus and the Pharisees.

Though Jesus came into the world as light to illuminate it, the world did not know Him. Isaiah wrote, "On that day the deaf will hear words of a book, and out of their gloom and darkness the eyes of the blind will see" (Isaiah 29:18). In Isaiah 35:5-6 we read, "Then the eyes of the blind will be opened and the ears of the deaf will be unstopped. Then the lame will leap like a dear, and the tongue of the mute will shout for joy." Moreover, in Isaiah 42:6-7 we read, "I am the LORD, I have called You in righteousness, I will also hold You by the hand and watch over You, and I will appoint You as a covenant to the people, as a light to the nations, to open blind eyes, to bring out prisoners from the dungeon and those who dwell in darkness from the prison." The light of the world brings light because He is light. What are you going to do with this information? Are you going to preach just a little sermon? The light of the world displays the radiant glory of God.

God's Glory Displayed

Though John 9 is a complicated narrative, the hinge of it all is in verse 3: "It was neither that this man sinned, nor his parents; but it was so that the works of God might be displayed in him." Now do we believe that or not? If we believe that, it makes all the difference in the world. A limitless universe of theology exists here. It is an earth-shaking reality. This man was born blind so that the works of God might be displayed in him.

The Pharisees were only the first to reject that theology. Preachers today look at this truth and explain away its threatening power. They domesticate it into a fascinating miracle account about Jesus the wonder worker. They moralize it by exhorting the blind to strain their eyes to see. They eviscerate it by denying the brute force of Jesus' words. They try to make it just mere literature filled with irony the literate love to enjoy. They apologize for it by explaining it as a crude theology that we have now overcome. They develop principles from it by offering a set of practical insights and observations for the wise and prudent. Or they transform it into therapy, encouraging all to abandon the unauthentic and find the sight of authenticity.

But Jesus said, "It was neither that this man sinned, nor his parents; but it was so that the works of God might be displayed in him." This is true about every one of us. It's true about every single human being who ever lived or will live. In fact, it's true about every atom and molecule of the cosmos. Why does anything exist? Why is anything as it is? Why is there anything at all? That the works of God might be displayed! This is way too much voltage for many. This means that in the ages past God determined that there would be a man who was blind. He was born blind so that Jesus would come along and spit into the ground, anoint the man's eyes, send him to wash, and he would come back seeing.

If you can handle that truth, then you can't preach a little sermon. There is no little moralism here. There aren't just a couple of principles here that we can apply. There is an entire universe of meaning that throws the world, as we know it, upside down. That's the reality of the gospel—it comes and mixes up our categories. It destroys all conventional wisdom. It tells us that we are blind and that God is working all things out for the display of His own glory. The great question is: Do we trust Him or not?

When this man had the opportunity to see Jesus, he did not ask, "Why was I blind?" Instead, he wanted to know who the Lord was. Christ is the light of the world who opened not only this man's eyes, but also the eyes of all who see Him as Savior and Lord. As a pastor, what will you do with this truth? Will you preach a little sermon? Shepherd, there are no little people. How many people do we pass every day who desperately need the gospel? Yet we do not see them.

There are no little texts, because all display the glory of God. If there are no little texts, then there must be no little sermons.

Jesus saw a man and healed him. May we see that there are no little people—only the fellow blind who desperately need sight. There must be no little sermons if we believe that every particle and every single human being exists so that the works of God may be displayed. There are no little people. There are no little texts, because all display the glory of God. If there are no little texts, then there must be no little sermons.

Billions of stars and all the infinitude of expanding space exist for one purpose alone: that God determined to save the people on this planet through the blood of His Son. The entire cosmos is nothing but a theater for the story of the drama of God's redemption. We know the secret to the universe. We know the secret to creation. We know the secret to the meaning of life. There is no excuse for any of us to keep saying, "I don't know." If you don't know, don't preach. If you don't know, find out. We know, so we preach. Since we know, there is no little text. And there are no little sermons.

If we understand this and establish our ministries on this, then we will never see a little person. We will never declare a little God. We will never proclaim a little gospel. We will never know a little truth. We will never work up a little message. We will never be driven by just a little conviction. We will never be fueled by just a little passion. We will never preach a little sermon. But if we don't believe this and stake our ministry on this, then just any little old sermon will do.

PRAYER

Our Father, we come before You to pray that there be no little sermons. We pray that You will use Your leaders to preach Your powerful Word. We pray to see Your glory in all endeavors and to see the miracle of the spiritually blind obtaining sight. To the glory of God, in the name of Jesus Christ our Lord, Amen.

Confronting Hypocrisy

"The Lord said to him, 'Now you Pharisees
clean the outside of the cup and of the platter;
but inside of you, you are full of robbery and wickedness.'"

Luke 11:39

10

CONFRONTING HYPOCRISY

John MacArthur
Shepherds' Conference 2005
Luke 11:37-44

It has been my heart's passion to call pastors to go to battle for the truth in a day in which we are losing it. From the very opening of Jude's letter we are called to earnestly contend for the faith which was once for all handed down to the saints, which is the basis of our common salvation. This command is a serious one, since certain persons have crept into the church unnoticed and are wreaking havoc on the truth; and this long war on the truth began with the fall of Satan and will go on until we reach the eternal state.

It is our time and our place in this world to be the warriors who defend the truth. While we can learn much from Jude about this, I want to take you to a completely different passage. I want to give you a glimpse of the greatest of all warriors for the truth, the Lord Jesus Christ, and how He dealt with one of the paramount enemies of the truth, hypocrisy.

The Encounter with a Hypocrite

In Luke chapter 11, we find an illustration in which Jesus confronted one of the many embedded spiritual terrorists of His day. This enemy was one of the many who had inserted themselves within the religious structure of Israel and had been accorded the highest place of respect and regard.

They were so effective and efficient that they were accepted and honored by everyone and were able to turn the whole nation against the long-awaited Messiah. In verses 37-44, we witness a meal that took place between Jesus and one of these spiritual enemies, a Pharisee.

> Now when He had spoken, a Pharisee asked Him to have lunch with him; and He went in, and reclined at the table. When the Pharisee saw it, he was surprised that He had not first ceremonially washed before the meal. But the Lord said to him, "Now you Pharisees clean the outside of the cup and of the plat-ter; but inside of you, you are full of robbery and wickedness. You foolish ones, did not He who made the outside make the inside also? But give that which is within as charity, and then all things are clean for you.

> "But woe to you Pharisees! For you pay tithe of mint and rue and every kind of garden herb, and yet disregard justice and the love of God; but these are the things you should have done without neglecting the others. Woe to you Pharisees! For you love the chief seats in the synagogues and the respectful greet-ings in the market places. Woe to you! For you are like con-cealed tombs, and the people who walk over them are unaware of it."

This is our great leader warring against a purveyor of error. For most readers it must seem strange that the most severe warnings and denunci-ations that Jesus Christ ever uttered were against the religious people of His day. In today's culture, we're supposed to embrace anybody and every-body who's religious, as if we were all engaged in worshiping and serving the same God. Since Jesus was, after all, a religious figure, it would seem that He would respect and affirm religious people more than anybody else, especially Jews who were devoted so fastidiously to the Old Testament law. But just the opposite was true.

The Disparagement of False Religion

Jesus, who is truth personified, perfectly understood true religion. He taught only what was true and what came from God, and understood damning deception when He saw it. Jesus knew what force in the world had the greatest power to destroy souls forever. He knew that of all the evils in the world, false religion—especially apostate Judaism and apostate Christianity—was the worst. The severest eternal judgment will be for the religious, especially those who pervert the Old and New Testaments.

Hebrews chapter 2 reveals that the judgment of God falls on those who have disregard for His law; and Hebrews 10 discloses that there is a horrific escalated judgment on those who disregard the New Testament and trample underfoot the blood of the covenant, counting it unholy and in some way perverting it. The leaders of the Jewish religion were apostates because they had perverted the Old Testament and rejected the Messiah and His salvation. These apostate leaders also manipulated the Romans into carrying out the execution of Christ that they themselves sought. Consequently, the Pharisees' judgment was to be severe, not only in a temporal sense with the destruction of Jerusalem, but in an eternal sense with the damnation of their souls.

Going back to Luke 11:29, we read that Jesus had been speaking to this crowd and said, "This generation is a wicked generation." Jesus was talking about the people of His own nation. Back in verse 14 of the same chapter, Jesus had cast a demon out of someone who had been made dumb by the demon. When the evil spirit came out, the dumb man spoke and the multitude marveled, while others said, "He casts out demons by Beelzebul, the ruler of the demons" (11:15). Since the populace was concluding that Jesus had supernatural power, there were only two options: either the power came from God, or it was from Satan. The crowds believed the Pharisees' lie that Jesus was from Satan, not God. They claimed that Jesus could not be from God because He contradicted the Pharisaical religious system, which was prescribed to be "from God." Their approach to religion was disastrous, and Jesus called them a wicked generation.

In verses 24-26, speaking to the same crowd, Jesus said,

> When the unclean spirit goes out of a man, it passes through waterless places seeking rest, and not finding any, it says, "I will return to my house from which I came." And when it comes, it finds it swept and put in order. Then it goes and takes along

seven other spirits more evil than itself, and they go in and live there; and the last state of that man becomes worse than the first.

Jesus taught that the worst possible condition a person can be in is to be moral and religious, but without God.

The Indictment of Hypocrisy

In another diatribe that Jesus pronounced on the Pharisees, He made it very clear how He viewed them: "Woe to you scribes and Pharisees, hypocrites because you travel around on sea and land to make one proselyte; and when he becomes one, you make him twice as much a son of hell as yourselves" (Matthew 23:15). In verse 33 He added, "You serpents, you brood of vipers, how will you escape the sentence of hell?" Pastor, if you are going to go to battle for the truth, then you have to confront the enemy.

The account in our text is a story of a religious Pharisee who was headed for hell. While on his way, he was making others "twice as much a son of hell" than he himself was. Like an extremist, he was taking the souls of others while condemning himself. Now, the Pharisees possessed moral sensitivities—apparently an active conscience, and strong religious convictions. Technically, they should have found some common ground and gotten along with Jesus, but just the opposite was true. Jesus said He was far more accepting of prostitutes, tax collectors, criminals, and the social riffraff than with the religious establishment. That was the case because Jesus did not come to call the righteous, but sinners to repentance.

Religion blinds people to the truth of their sin, makes them self-righteous, feeds pride, fuels vanity, and produces skilled hypocrites. The Pharisees were the most devout among the Jews and were the main spiritual models for the people, yet their warped and distorted interpretation of the Old Testament not only cut themselves off from God, but others as well. I do not think all the Pharisees sought to be hypocrites, but that is how it turns out when you are religious on the outside and evil on the inside. False religion forces an individual to become skilled at covering corruption and adept at external morality and ritual so as to carry on a deception. The Pharisees had no love for God, knew no power from the Holy Spirit, had no knowledge of the truth, and possessed absolutely no righteousness. They were actors and, like all hypocrites, the more they did it, the more convincing they became.

The Pharisees were very good at faking religion. We read in Matthew 23:13, "Woe to you...hypocrites...for you do not enter in yourselves, nor do you allow those who are entering to go in." Verse 15 adds, "You travel around on sea and land to make one proselyte; and when he becomes one, you make him twice as much a son of hell as yourselves." They cared about the little ritualistic details and neglected big moral issues (23:23). Jesus said, "You clean the outside, not the inside" (see verse 25). And in verse 27 He said, "You are like whitewashed tombs." The Pharisees provided superficial homage to the prophets, but they did not care about righteousness (verse 29). Jesus completely exposed these false leaders using the most incisive and graphic language.

As pastors, we need to remember that we have an obligation not to accept false teachers, but to evangelize them.

A Lesson on Confronting Hypocrisy

Though Jesus confronted hypocrites, He did so with a merciful purpose in mind. As pastors, we need to remember that we have an obligation not to accept false teachers, but to evangelize them. In Luke 11:37-44, Jesus taught us how to confront a religious deceiver. But this lesson does not entail that the response will always be positive, for Jesus' situation with the Pharisees did not end well: "When [Jesus] left there, the scribes and the Pharisees began to be very hostile and to question Him closely on many subjects, plotting against Him to catch Him in something He might say" (verses 53-54).

We see how our Lord mercifully confronted the Pharisees to expose their true condition. Contrary to Jesus' approach, in our modern day, evangelicals are quick to embrace false religionists and hypocrites. It is as if there were some ground to be gained in doing this, but all that evangelicals are doing is aiding and abetting the damnation of hypocrites. As students of God's Word, we have the responsibility to confront false teachers about their own condition. Religious hypocrites have unchanged hearts, are cut off from God, and are left to define their religion and their spirituality by what they do externally. These individuals do not need cover; they need confrontation.

The Pharisees' religion was external, and when all you have is the external, then you expand on it. They expanded the ceremonies, the rituals, and the prescriptions. They had nothing on the inside, so they took the basic law of God in the Old Testament and they inflated it by adding to it until it was beyond comprehension. This is essentially what the Roman Catholic system has done—adding endless regulations, supposed revelations, and requirements to further define their godliness by giving attention to ceremonial minutia. Therefore, to expose their true condition is perceived as an attack on their system. Jesus did exactly that when in Luke chapter 11 He launched His confrontation with the Pharisee. Jesus' strategy was to step right into the situation and immediately violate the man's conventions.

"When he had spoken" indicates that Jesus had completed His teaching to the multitude, in which He told them what a wicked generation they were and how they had plenty of light but no sight (Luke 11:37). After this talk, a Pharisee asked Jesus to have a meal with him. Pharisees were not priests, but laymen who were extremely devoted to the law and tradition. They had effectively obscured the law by adding to it. They had become known as the spiritual authorities in Israel to whom the people looked. And by Jesus' time, they were self-righteous, evil, degenerate, hypocritical, filled with pride, and abusive to the people.

One of them, for reasons that are not disclosed, invited Jesus to eat with him. This is shocking because the animosity between the Pharisees and Jesus had already been made evident. In fact, the Pharisees had even begun plotting Jesus' death. Yet there is no indication that this Pharisee in Luke 11:37 had an evil motive, and there is no indication what his motive was.

Now in ancient Israel, there were two main meals—a late morning lunch, and a late afternoon dinner. This man invited Jesus to come and have lunch with him. This event started off innocently because Jesus agreed to the invitation, came in, and reclined (verse 37). The usual posture for somebody who was going to eat at a social meal was the reclined position. There would be a couch or elongated place to sit, and guests would come to stay, recline, converse, and eat. For someone to invite a guest in this way was so that the people involved could get to know one another. It is at this point in the narrative that we learn the characteristics of false religion and hypocrisy.

The Characteristics of Hypocrisy

A Love of the Symbolic

The first characteristic of false religion is that it loves the symbolic. This is not true in just this case; it's generally true in every false religion. Whether you're discussing the Roman Catholic Church, the Greek Orthodox, or whatever other false religion, you learn that reality is absent and symbols are substituted. "When the Pharisee saw it, he was surprised that [Jesus] had not first ceremonially washed before the meal" (11:38). Jesus purposely walked right in, went to the table, and reclined. He knew what was expected of Him, and He did not do it. He knew the expected ritual, for He had been raised in that culture. As a result, the Pharisee was surprised—literally amazed—that Jesus had not first ceremonially washed.

The key word here is "ceremonially." The issue was not with dirt or hygiene, but with a ceremonial symbol developed in Judaistic practice. In case a Jew had touched a Gentile that day, or touched something a Gentile had touched, or had touched something unclean, he was required to symbolize the desire to be clean of all defiling contacts in the world by ceremonially washing himself.

According to Jewish tradition, there were certain ways the washing was to be done. But can these details be found in the Old Testament? No, because they have nothing to do with the Old Testament. This was an empty act of ceremonial purity that did nothing for the corruption of the heart. That is exactly what Jesus was talking about in Matthew 15 when He said that the religious leaders had substituted the traditions of men for the commandments of God. They could not keep the commandments of God, so they invented foolish traditions.

Jesus walked in, sat down, and in effect said, "I'm not interested in your symbols, and I don't want to belong to your club." Jesus was willing to insult the man in order to confront his spiritual condition. The man was obsessed with symbols because false religion is stuck on symbols. Hypocrites have a love for the symbolic.

A Love of the Sinful

The second characteristic of false religion is a love of the sinful. Though Jesus and the Pharisee had not said anything yet, Jesus knew exactly what the Pharisee was thinking. The Pharisee just stood there in shock because Jesus had not taken water and dribbled it across his fingers (Luke 11:38). Did the Lord say to the man, "Thanks for inviting me to lunch"? No. Did He say, "It's nice to meet you. So glad you're religious. You know we worship the same God, Jehovah"? He did not say any of that. Rather, He said, "Now you Pharisees clean the outside of the cup and of the platter; but inside of you, you are full of robbery and wickedness" (verse 39). Jesus instantly got to the heart of the matter and exposed that the Pharisee actually loved what was sinful. Jesus read the man's mind; the man was troubled by Jesus rejecting the symbolic, so Jesus immediately and unapologetically confronted the man's superficiality.

Jesus' choice of analogy was a very good one, since they were sitting at a table ready to have lunch. Whoever heard of washing just the outside of a dish when it is the inside that holds the food? It is pointless to wash only the outside and put the food on the inside. Jesus implied that this man was clean where it didn't matter. The ritualistic washing may have cleaned the outside of the body, but inside, he was "full of robbery and wickedness" (verse 39). The word "robbery," means to plunder, pillage, rape, to take something violently by force. The Pharisees were pillaging people's lives and abusing them as spiritual terrorists. Jesus also mentioned that the Pharisee was full of "wickedness," which entails an evil disposition, since its synonym is villain.

The more I study the Gospels, the more impressed I am with the direct approach that Jesus used. Jesus saw that this man was like the false prophets before him, who devoured the poor, plied their hypocrisy for personal gain, and abused people's souls. This hypocrite had a love for the sinful.

A Love of the Simplistic

The third characteristic of false religion and hypocrisy is that it loves the simplistic. Jesus insightfully continued, "You foolish ones, did not He who made the outside make the inside also?" (verse 40). The Pharisees were ceremonialists who were shallow in their theology. It is necessary to clarify here that something that is simple has a clear meaning and is not complex. However, *simplistic* means to be overly and irrationally simple. One has to be a fool to be in a false religion and to be a purveyor of it, because he lives with the simplistic reality that God only cares about the outside. The Greek word translated "foolish ones" could be stretched to mean "you brainless ones," or "you simpletons." The Pharisees were destitute of the knowledge of the truth and lived their lives before the God they claimed to worship, thinking He would be satisfied with the outside and not concerned about the inside. Hypocrites know what they are on the inside. In 1 Corinthians 2:11, Paul wrote, "Who among men knows the thoughts of a man except the spirit of a man which is in him?" Everyone knows their own heart. To be a human being means that you are self-conscious and know what's going on inside of you.

It's axiomatic to say that the spirit of a man knows what's in a man. Therefore, why would anyone think that a holy God is content with an individual being ceremonially clean with no regard for the inside? It certainly wouldn't seem to be a leap of intelligence to understand that if the Creator was concerned about the outside, He was also concerned about the inside. How ridiculous and sophomoric were these Pharisees? They were supposed to be teachers of deep divine truth, to know God, to be righteous, and to be the standard of virtue and holiness. And yet they thought that God was not interested in what was going on in their wretched hearts. Paul wrote in Romans 2:29, "He is a Jew who is one inwardly; and circumcision is that which is of the heart." Even the Jews knew that God cared about the internal.

In Luke 11:41, Jesus continued, "Give that which is within as charity, and then all things are clean for you." Jesus basically told the man to take care of his heart—to let his heart go out to the poor and those in need. It is as if Jesus were saying, "You've got all your superficial almsgiving, all your phony prayers, all your phony fasts, all your hypocritical ceremonies, and yet you plunder people for the sake of self-gain. You use, and abuse, and rob them blind. You can't believe God doesn't care about your heart."

The Pharisees weren't alone in loving the simplistic. That still happens today. For example, ask yourself how a Roman Catholic priest can be so simplistic as to go around wearing the garb, partaking in all the ceremonies and rituals, representing himself as a holy man of God, and going out and being sexually immoral as a way of life?

In the Pharisees' case it might not have been sexual immorality, but it definitely involved devouring the poor and abusing people. How does one not go mad with guilt to stand and portray himself as a holy person and be in habitual sin? Sadly, this is an epidemic in every false religion because the heart has never changed. And there are even men who preach the true gospel who become very adept hypocrites. The longer they do it, the more skilled they become, and the more they quiet their conscience, the bigger the disaster is when it finally becomes known. So we must remember that God is the God of the inside and the outside. We cannot be simplistic like the Pharisees.

A Love of the Secondary

The fourth characteristic of religious hypocrites is that they love the secondary. Note Jesus' rebuke in verse 42: "Woe to you Pharisees! For you pay tithe of mint and rue and every kind of garden herb, and yet disregard justice and the love of God; but these are the things you should have done without neglecting the others." Now, it is important to remember that Jesus had been invited to lunch so the man could find out more about Jesus. But Jesus unmasked this man's love of the symbolic, sinful, and simplistic. In the next three verses Jesus pronounced three curses on the man—and not just on this Pharisee, but on all Pharisees. Jesus made the diagnosis instantly, and He pronounced the judgment almost as instantly.

"Woe" has already been used in the Gospel of Luke on several occasions against cities upon which our Lord pronounced judgment. "Woe" is not a sentiment of sorrow; it is a declaration of judgment. In Mathew 23, Jesus said "woe" multiple times as He spoke to the sons of hell who were headed for destruction, and who would have a greater condemnation. Therefore, when Jesus said "woe" in Luke 11, He spoke a word of judgment on this man. Why? "You pay tithe of mint and rue and every kind of garden herb, and yet disregard justice and the love of God" (verse 42).

The Pharisees did not understand what was primary, and loved the secondary. Like all religious people who don't know God, the Pharisees did only the external things they could do, and not those things that stem from the heart. The Old Testament required that a tenth of a person's grain, wine, oil, and flock be given to the Levites (Deuteronomy 14). Another tenth was to be provided for the national feast (Leviticus 27). Also, every third year, another tenth was to be given for the poor (Deuteronomy 26). All this giving was intended to help fund the theocracy, but there was no command in the Old Testament to tithe at this Pharisaical minute level. Can you imagine going to the temple with a bag of seeds and dropping one out of every ten seeds into a receptacle? In fact, the Mishnah states that the condiments like salt were exempt from the tithe. The Pharisees' observations were ridiculous!

The Pharisees had no heart for justice and no heart for God. They could not love the Lord their God with any part of their heart, any part of their mind, any part of their soul, or any part of their strength. Nor could they love their neighbor as themselves. Instead, they fussed with what did not matter, and fiddled with the minutia.

A Love of Status

The fifth characteristic of hypocritical religion is a love of status. We read in verse 43, "Woe to you Pharisees! For you love the chief seats in the synagogues and the respectful greetings in the market places." False religious leaders love being accorded reverences, elevated positions, veneration, and admiration. They seek long, drawn-out designations that somehow give them higher esteem with the people. The chief seats in the synagogues faced the congregation, and these leaders sat there for everyone to witness their splendor. They desired to promote themselves.

In Mathew 23:5-12 we learn that these men loved to be called father, Rabbi, and teacher. They loved to be greeted in the marketplace. Yet their desire for status in the people's eyes was a form of idolatry. In John 5:44 our Lord asked the Jewish leaders, "How can you believe, when you receive glory from one another and you do not seek the glory that is from the one and only God?" Now that is the picture of false religious leaders—they claim to love God, love people, have insight into spirituality and religion, be holy and righteous and virtuous, but in reality all they care about is receiving glory and praise from people. They are spiritual terrorists who literally take people to hell with them.

Jesus concluded this indictment in Luke 11:44: "Woe to you! For you are like concealed tombs, and the people who walk over them are unaware of it." The Lord was saying, "I pronounce damnation on you because of what you do to the people who get near you." This time the judgment was not of their own evil, but of the evil transmitted to others. The whole nation of Israel had bought into their lies and hypocrisy. They followed in the same wickedness, and their end was the same judgment.

Jesus used the analogy of tombs because the Old Testament prohibited Israelites from touching a dead body (Leviticus 21). If a person touched a corpse, he was considered ceremonially defiled and could not observe the Passover according to Numbers 29. To become clean once again, he had to participate in ceremonial purification. In fact, Numbers 19 describes a seven-day purification process that was a nuisance to carry out. Because of the law's prohibitions, all graves were marked to ensure that no one accidently touched them. Tombs were whitewashed so that people wouldn't go near them and be defiled.

**Those of us who serve in the ministry must learn Jesus'
model for confronting evil for the merciful sake of the person
who is the purveyor of evil.**

Jesus said that the Pharisees were like an unmarked grave. People came in contact with them and had no idea that they were being defiled. And the defilement they experienced was not only ceremonial, but spiritual as well because their soul was in harm's way. Jesus knew how critical it was to address this issue. Mercifully, He gave this Pharisee every opportunity to see himself for who he really was, but in the end, the response was hostility (Luke 11:53).

The Responsibility to Expose Hypocrisy

Those of us who serve in the ministry must learn Jesus' model for confronting evil for the merciful sake of the person who is the purveyor of evil. We have a responsibility to expose that person to himself as well as to others. Jesus' meeting began as a private one, but He took it from there and expanded it to the larger group, and later the larger group got the message and was duly confronted.

We also need to make sure we do not become anything like these men. We do not want to get caught up in symbols; we want to be the real thing. We do not want to live in some simplistic kind of schizophrenia where we carry on self-deception by being clean on the outside, while on the inside our minds and hearts are full of sin. We do not want to spend our lives fiddling around with secondary issues and rearranging deck chairs on the Titanic. We do not want to fool with what does not matter. We do not want to be guilty of seeking status, exaltation, or glory. Rather, we must be those who love righteousness, love God, love Christ, love biblical truth, love others, and love lowliness and humility. So that those who are under our charge, when they bump into us, are not defiled and exposed to death, but to life.

PRAYER

Father, we thank You for Your Word and the opportunity to witness this Pharisee's lunch with our Lord. We see Jesus as a solitary figure with the whole nation against Him. He was the only One able to fight the battle to expose deceivers and to unmask the spiritual terrorists. Our Savior was always merciful to tell the truth about someone's spiritual condition. May we go forth in the spirit of our Lord Jesus to bring compassion to the broken sinner, and confrontation to the religious hypocrites. Help us speak the truth in love with mercy, but also to hold nothing back. Protect us from being hypocrites, living one way before our people and another way before You. We want to stand with our Savior in whose name we pray, Amen.

What Is Missing from Your Church Service?

"Until I come, give attention to the
public reading of Scripture,
to exhortation and teaching."

1 Timothy 4:13

11

WHAT IS MISSING FROM YOUR CHURCH SERVICE?

Austin T. Duncan
Shepherds' Conference 2014
Selected Scriptures

What is missing from your church service? Is it a fresh approach to welcoming visitors, new songs on the set list, or a need to revisit the ban on coffee in the auditorium? Your church may miss these things, but new songs, coffee, and a new announcement guy are not integral to a biblical church service. Although most congregants in America observe baptism, partake of the elements, sing together, and sit under preaching, they often forget two key elements to a biblical church service: the public reading of Scripture and pastoral prayer. Scripture commends these forms of worship, which are not only biblical but tremendously beneficial to your congregation. As pastors, we must strive to benefit our people by publicly reading God's Word and corporately praying to God in compelling and effective ways.

The Problem

When public reading of Scripture happens, pastors often carry it out without proper care, regard, or attention. Few take into consideration oral interpretation, producing sloppy readers of Scripture whose helter-skelter reading conveys an equally sloppy view of Scripture. Church leaders deliver announcements with more flourish than they do when reading God's matchless Word. When it comes to congregational prayer, churchgoers experience "free for all" intercession for Aunt Edna's narcoleptic cataplexy, or things of that nature. Sometimes corporate prayer becomes a gossip session, a more spiritual version of church announcements, or a WebMD catalog of illnesses. As pastors, we need to be more effective in these areas, for the ingredients of our worship services are not up to us but are ultimately established by God. Corporate reading thunders God's voice, and pastoral prayer moves mountains. In short, they matter.

Public Reading of Scripture: Biblical Support

Geoffrey Kirkland writes, "The public reading of Scripture is the reverential, repetitive, corporate and audible reading from the word of God in the regular gathering of believers for the purpose of reinforcing what God has said, recommitting one's self to obedience, and recognizing both the holiness of God and the holiness that God demands from His worshipers."[1]

The key words are *reverential, repetitive, corporate,* and *audible.* This public reading is distinct from the reading of the text for the sermon.

In Deuteronomy 31:9-13, Moses inaugurated a pattern of public reading of Scripture:

> So Moses wrote this law and gave it to the priests, the sons of Levi who carried the ark of the covenant of the LORD, and to all the elders of Israel. Then Moses commanded them, saying, "At the end of every seven years, at the time of the year of remission of debts, at the Feast of Booths, when all Israel comes to appear before the LORD your God at the place which He will choose, you shall read this law in front of all Israel in their hearing. Assemble the people, the men and the women and children and the alien who is in your town, so that they may hear and learn and fear the LORD your God, and be careful to observe all the words of this law. Their children, who have not known, will hear and learn to fear the LORD your God, as long as you live on the land which you are about to cross the Jordan to possess."

Before Israel entered Canaan, Moses prescribed regular reading of the Torah to ensure their covenant faithfulness. The people needed to be exposed to the Book of the Law by regularly hearing the reading of the Word. To hear the Word was a reminder that the source of this Word was not the people or even their leadership, but God. And though future generations would not hear God's voice audibly like the former generation did in Sinai, they would still hear His voice in His revelatory Word. The goal of public Scripture reading was to preserve the Israelites as a holy people, always dependent on the Word of God.

Throughout the momentous events in the life of Israel, the tradition of audibly reading the Word of God continued in Exodus, Joshua, and Nehemiah. The Psalms too commend audible reading, since certain psalms are intended to be antiphonal or for responsive reading. Antiphonal reading is done with two groups of people speaking or singing to each other different parts of the Psalms. Like a musical duet, priests and the people of Israel together sing praises to the Lord. In Deuteronomy 27 and Joshua 8, the people recount God's words to each other. The reading of the Word was a confession of the truth, a reinforcing of the covenant and a reminder of the importance of God's revelation to his people.

Between the Testaments, synagogues formed in which God's people assembled and followed a scheduled reading. Everett Ferguson writes, "The synagogue service included Scripture readings, interspersed with psalms, chants, sermons, prayers, alms-giving. We find the same elements in the early accounts of Christian worship, reading, singing, preaching, praying and giving."[2] That sounds very much like a church service.

In Luke 4, Jesus the Rabbi opened the scroll of Isaiah, reading powerfully from God's Word and saying, "Today this Scripture has been fulfilled in your hearing" (verse 21). That was not an unusual practice; it was the norm for the worship conducted in Jesus' day.

The New Testament practice of Scripture reading continued after the resurrection of Christ. First Timothy 4:13 reads, "Until I come, give attention to the public reading of Scripture, to exhortation and teaching." Without getting overly technical, a case can be made that this passage is not about merely reading a passage for the sake of exposition, but instituting a separate practice that was to be done by the Christians. The most obvious evidence for this is that there are three elements listed here: the public reading of Scripture, exhortation, and teaching. Three clearly separate elements are identified, and Paul exhorted Timothy to apply himself to doing all three in the context of pastoral ministry. This is how Phillip Towner describes it: "A community practice designed to steer the congregation out of the unorthodox backwaters of the heretical reading of certain texts, and back into the mainstream of the biblical story."[3] The people were prone to falling for myths and apocryphal tales, and Timothy was commanded to read the Scriptures so that the people would stay true to the Word of God.

The epistles provide further examples of the early church reading Scripture publicly. Christians shared these letters among churches, read them aloud in their gatherings, and treated them as Scripture. Peter confirmed that the apostolic writings were on par with the Old Testament (2 Peter 3:16), and Christians were to continue reading the Old Testament as well as the apostolic epistles in order to know the full revelation of God (Ephesians 5:19; Colossians 3:16). This is reason enough for us to engage in the public reading of Scripture.

Public Reading of Scripture: The Benefits

Not only is the public reading of Scripture biblical, it is also beneficial. Let's look at four benefits the public reading of Scripture provides.

Combats the Anemic Use of Scripture

First, reading Scripture publicly energizes your use of Scripture. When you open God's Word and you read it without a comment, introduction, or necessary explanation, it reinforces what you believe about Scripture when you hear Scripture that is from God. There is a difference between a church service that focuses on solely horizontal aspects of worship and a church service that fixes its gaze vertically by intentionally hearing from God.

There is a reverence that comes from the plain reading of God's Word that just doesn't fit in most worship services, because most worship services are concerned with not overwhelming the congregation with the

Bible. Pastors don't want to distract from the message they have prepared or their zingy introduction. Such actions show that a church's leadership does not understand the nature and power of Scripture. Your doctrine of Scripture is weak if you don't have room for the public reading of Scripture. The practice of reading Scripture publicly connects the church body to Scripture and to a robust doctrine of Scripture by giving them an awareness of the power of the Word.

The churches I grew up in and served in before I came to Grace Community Church never did this. So the first time my wife and I attended Grace Community Church, we listened to Pastor MacArthur open the Bible and read through an entire chapter. This reading was immediately followed by a lengthy pastoral prayer that was focused and sobering. At first I wasn't used to so much standing, but it was clear that comments like, "Ladies and gentlemen, let's hear you make some noise for Jesus," or "Put your hands together for the Lord" would not fit in such a setting. When one hears the sustained reading of the Word of God, it forces him to realize that this church holds the Word of God in high regard.

The public reading of God's Word directs the entire service toward the God who speaks in Scripture.

Pastor, when you implement this practice into your worship service, and do it well, it teaches your people to love the Word of God and to depend on Scripture alone. It has the double-edged effect of Hebrews 4:12. It reminds us that we are not central. The Word of God can and will work apart from our expository insights. A story from C.H. Spurgeon's life illustrates this double-edged effect. When Spurgeon was testing the acoustics of the Crystal Palace in London, he climbed up into the pulpit and said, "Behold the Lamb of God, which taketh away the sin of the world" (John 1:29 KJV). A workman who was in one of the galleries heard this declaration and was soundly converted. This serves as a reminder of the inherent power of the Word of God. Does the effectiveness of

Scripture make you less important? Yes! And isn't it great that the power is not in you?

The public reading of God's Word directs the entire service toward the God who speaks in Scripture. It reminds us that revelation itself is a mercy. It shows the power of God to save and always accomplish His purpose (Isaiah 55:10-11). It confronts the sin in a congregation (James 1:23-25). Though you may not be preaching on sexual immorality during a given week, perhaps there's someone in the congregation who needs to hear a warning about that specific sin and your reading of 1 Thessalonians 4 addresses it. Praise God in His providence that He has a word for your people that you did not prepare!

Yet many evangelical churches send the reading of Scripture to boarding school, keeping it out of sight and mind. "It's ironic," writes one author, "that among even evangelicals, the people who above all see themselves as Bible people, there is so little enthusiasm for the public reading of the Bible."[4] But reading the Bible is powerful because we believe in the perspicuity of Scripture; we believe the Scripture is inherently clear. David F. Wells, in his book *God in the Wasteland*, speaks on the issue of inerrancy:

> The issue of inherency basically focuses on the *nature* of the Bible. It is entirely possible for those who have sworn to defend the concept of biblical inherency to function as if they had no such word in their hands. Indeed it happens all the time. And the sad fact is that when the nature of the Bible was being debated, the Bible itself was quietly falling into disuse in the church...Without this transcendent Word in its life, the church has no rudder, no compass, no provisions. Without the Word it has no capacity to stand outside its culture, to detect and wrench itself free from the seductions of modernity. Without the Word the church has no meaning.[5]

Cures Historical Amnesia

Second, reading Scripture aloud cures historical amnesia. Ferguson writes, "It must be remembered that the principal opportunity for most Christians to become acquainted with the Scriptures was through hearing them read in the church."[6] Therefore the regular consecutive reading of the Bible occupied a key place in the early church's history. Obviously, the early church did not have a personal leather-bound or quilted-covered copy of Scripture. The congregants did not have a stack of Bibles at home. Instead, they listened to the reading of Scripture when they gathered. The public reading of Scripture is not just a personal practice but a community practice that has been done throughout the history of the church.

Public reading was first done in the synagogue, and as soon as the apostolic age was over, we witness the testimony of a man like Justin Martyr, who wrote, "On the day which is called Sunday, an assembly of believers, through town and country, takes place upon some common spot, where the writings of the apostles, or the books of the prophets, are publicly read so long as the time allows." That was written in approximately AD 158. As you continue through church history, in the fourth century there emerges a dominant liturgical pattern that includes multiple readings: one from the Old Testament and two from the Gospels. During the final reading, the people would stand. Now, I'm not calling the church to emulate these particulars of the historical tradition. Rather, I want to point out why our churches look so different from churches a thousand years ago and even hundreds of years ago. For 2000 years, the church observed the public reading of Scripture. Where did the practice go?

The church today is preoccupied with making an awesome contemporary video for Father's Day or putting a bed on the rooftop to promote a series on marital intimacy. It's what Thomas Bergler writes about in his book *The Juvenilization of American Christianity*. He calls the modern-day church a youth group on steroids. I'm not condemning youth groups, but there is something to be said about letting our corporate worship time be prescribed by God instead of culture. We need to seek to please God in our worship, not pander to the lowest common denominator. Church history can expose our folly and show us a more mature way. Christians have been reading the Bible in their worship services for 2000 years; there are many more examples of the public reading of Scripture in church history (see Bryan Chapell, *Christ-Centered Worship* 2nd ed. [Grand Rapids, MI: Baker, 2009], pp. 220-33). Let's not trade that heritage for a Fourth of July slideshow.

Cornerstone to Expository Preaching

Third, the public reading of Scripture constitutes the cornerstone to expository preaching. Preaching begins with learning to read your Bible aloud. The first time I listened to Pastor MacArthur preach, I was shocked by how he read the Bible. I could tell that he understood what it meant. Before he got into any explanation or before he gave any outline, he provided interpretation even with how he paused and emphasized certain portions of the passage. I'm also reminded of a Shepherds' Conference that took place approximately ten years ago when Mark Dever was here. He read from Ezekiel chapter 1 and I was undone like Ezekiel by just hearing the passage read. In their readings of Scripture, it was clear that both of these men held the Word in high regard. The cornerstone of good preaching is good reading.

Jeffery D. Arthurs, in his book *Devote Yourself to the Public Reading of Scripture,* writes, "In many churches, public reading of the Bible is little more than homiletical throat-clearing before the sermon."[7] When you read the Scripture without explanation, you are saying something about the foundational and revelatory nature of Scripture. As expositors, we of all people ought to have confidence that God's Word can speak for itself. And that is precisely what it does during the public reading of Scripture.

Counters the Man-Centered Service

Fourth, reading Scripture publicly counters a man-centered service. It cultivates the reverence and sobriety that I've already mentioned. A church that reads the Word is a church that is pointed toward heaven. What a joy it is to be under the spoken Word in the presence of other people who are saying, "We submit to this holy Word. This is our guide. This is our God. He has spoken." This isn't something you can livestream.

Public Reading of Scripture: How to Do It Well

So that we might do well at the public reading of Scripture, I want to provide a few tips.

Read for Interpretation

The *first* tip is to read for interpretation. A member of the orchestra does not determine the speed or the meter of a piece of music before him.

The speed and the meter are written in the music and guided by the conductor. The musician is called upon to faithfully interpret the genius who wrote the piece. Likewise, the one who reads Scripture publicly must give expression to the author's intent and convey the message that's set before him.

For example, Luke 2:16 says, "And they went with haste [long pause], and found Mary and Joseph, and the baby lying in a manger" (ESV). If the second half of that sentence is read too fast without a pause, it sounds like Mary, Joseph, and Jesus were all lying in the manger. That's a big trough. If the text is read wrong, the interpretation is wrong. Let's try it again: "And they went with haste, and found Mary and Joseph [long pause], and the baby lying in a manger." Now it is evident that only Jesus was lying in the manger. By reading well, the pastor provides interpretation and teaches his people good hermeneutics—to mind the paragraph, to mind the punctuation, and to mind the grammar.

A pastor can fail to group words or phrases properly, or even miss the tone of the text. He needs to make climactic what the writer intended to make climactic and to show feeling appropriate for the sense of the passage. This is what oral interpretation is about, and it used to be a fundamental component of any seminary curriculum that intentionally taught preachers to read before teaching them to preach. Reading well is a tool for discovering the treasures that are in the passage. You note things like genre as you read a narrative with movement and emotion. You read poetry mindful of its beauty and symmetry. In Psalm 18, you want to convey the terror and awe of the theophany. Psalm 3 begins with despair, leads to confidence, and ends with assurance. As you read God's Word, you can convey those varying emotions and you don't have to have your Screen Actors Guild card to figure out how to relay assurance when you read, because if you have a heart of faith, you already understand the comfort assurance brings. This is not putting on a show, but reading with interpretation.

In reading the epistles, you emphasize the verbs, follow the arguments, and articulate the writer's ironclad logic. You have to understand the text if you're going to read it well, and you can't fake it. A pastor cannot just get up and rely on his giftedness, because when he gets to Romans chapter 16, he's in trouble if he doesn't know how to greet Tryphaena, Tryphosa, Asyncritus, and Phlegon. When you don't take time to pronounce properly, ultimately, you teach your people that there is irreverence and lack of concern with regard to certain aspects of Scripture. As a preacher, you have to remember that even the genealogies are included in Scripture by God, and are useful for teaching, rebuking, correcting, and training in righteousness.

Read Prepared

This leads me to the *second* tip: Be prepared. Do not fake, wing, or ad-lib a reading. One has to study to read publicly, just like he has to study to present a sermon. The pastor has to let the message soak in, to understand it, and to own it. This may not entail memorizing the passage, but rather, gaining a deep familiarity of the text. Keep in mind the tricky bits, obey the punctuation, and use tools that will help you to know the meaning and the pronunciation of certain words.

Read as a Believer

The *third* tip is to read as a believer. Stephen Olford wrote, "Read it as though you believe it."[8] Faith, assurance, and confidence must be in your voice to stress that you believe in the sufficiency of Scripture. After all, you are reading the Word of God, and the Word is true, sure, and reliable. Read the Bible in such a way that you exemplify trust in the author (see Psalm 19:7-9).

Read with Appropriate Awareness

The *fourth* tip is to read with an appropriate awareness of yourself. This means being mindful of your body, your head, your face, your arms, your hands, and even your feet. Gestures ought to be natural and may need regulation when they're unhelpful. Some preachers look like they're being attacked by a swarm of bees. If you struggle with this, then enlist a helper, someone who will speak the truth to you. Don't say, "Come to Me, all who are weary and heavy-laden, and I will give you rest" (Matthew 11:28) while you put your arms forward, palms facing outward in a stopping motion. That distancing gesture does not convey the welcoming tone of that passage. Again, the goal is to be natural, mindful, appropriate, and prevent from being distracting. As you preach, make sure you carry out the task in a way that it's not about you, but about the Scripture.

Chapell says it this way: "The reader of Scriptures...is the most conspicuous component in the transmission of the Word, and at the same time the least important character in the spiritual drama between God and the assembled audience."[9] This is a good reminder to remove yourself from the experience. It's not about you, and it's not about your skill as a reader. It's about getting out of the way and enabling your people to hear God's Word unmixed with anything else.

Practice Reading

The *fifth* and final tip is to practice reading. I would encourage you to listen to a recording of yourself, which may be excruciatingly painful. But if you never do it, then you won't find out your verbal tics. As you practice reading, read in a normal and natural tone of voice—responsibly, respectfully, and reliably. Read with meaning, sympathy, real expression, and emphasis. Read with expectation, humble submission, and confident faith. Good preachers are plentiful compared to good readers. To become a good reader will require practice.

Allen Ross summarizes the matter well in *Recalling the Hope of Glory*:

> The reading of Scripture and the exposition of it are primary acts of worship in the church; they are offerings given to God in reverence and devotion. Reading God's holy Word in the assembly without understanding, interpretation, or enthusiasm undermines the foundation of all worship, which is to hear from God. When the reading of Scripture is with clarity, conviction, and power, it sets the Word of God before the people in a way that demonstrates its authority and demands a response. The reading of Scripture should be one of the most powerful parts of worship—every word spoken from the Word is from God.[10]

The public reading of Scripture is neglected in many churches today, but I don't know if it's as neglected as leading in pastoral prayer.

Pastoral Prayer: Biblical Support

Corporate pastoral prayer is directly connected with the public reading of Scripture because it is another aspect of worship that is prescribed by

God. The biblical support for this is extensive. In 1 Kings chapter 8, Solomon prayed at the completion of the temple. The corporate nature of the prayer is evident by the use of plural pronouns us, our, and we:

> When Solomon had finished praying this entire prayer and supplication to the LORD, he arose from before the altar of the LORD, from kneeling on his knees with his hands spread toward heaven. And he stood and blessed all the assembly of Israel with a loud voice, saying: "Blessed be the LORD, who has given rest to His people Israel, according to all that He promised; not one word has failed of all His good promise, which He promised through Moses His servant. May the LORD our God be with us, as He was with our fathers; may He not leave us or forsake us, that He may incline our hearts to Himself, to walk in all His ways and to keep His commandments and His statutes and His ordinances, which He commanded our fathers. And may these words of mine, with which I have made supplication before the LORD, be near to the LORD our God day and night, that He may maintain the cause of His servant and the cause of His people Israel, as each day requires, so that all the peoples of the earth may know that the LORD is God; there is no one else. Let your heart therefore be wholly devoted to the LORD our God, to walk in His statutes and to keep His commandments, as at this day."

This powerful benediction was not focused on Solomon, but on Solomon and Israel together as the recipients of God's blessing. This type of prayer is also evident as the prophet Ezra prays for the people of Israel in 1 Chronicles 29 and Ezra chapters 9 through 10. Then in the New Testament, we read in Acts 2:42 that the people of God were dedicated to praying together. In today's individualistic society, we are often thoughtful toward our individual responsibility to read the Bible, pray, and have times of devotion and solitude. Yet the far greater emphasis in the Scriptures is toward corporate spiritual disciplines and corporate prayer. And in Acts 4:23-31, it is clear what kind of prayer meetings the early church experienced. Believers were not praying about Aunt Bertha's chronic liver issues. Instead, we read,

When they had been released, they went to their own companions and reported all that the chief priests and the elders had said to them. And when they heard this, they lifted their voices to God with one accord and said, "O Lord, it is You who made the heaven and the earth and the sea, and all that is in them, who by the Holy Spirit, through the mouth of our father David Your servant, said, 'Why did the Gentiles rage, and the peoples devise futile things? The kings of the earth took their stand, and the rulers were gathered together against the Lord and against His Christ.' For truly in this city there were gathered together against Your holy servant Jesus, whom You anointed, both Herod and Pontius Pilate, along with the Gentiles and the peoples of Israel, to do whatever Your hand and Your purpose predestined to occur. And now, Lord, take note of their threats, and grant that Your bond-servants may speak Your word with all confidence, while You extend Your hand to heal, and signs and wonders take place through the name of Your holy servant Jesus." And when they had prayed, the place where they had gathered together was shaken, and they were all filled with the Holy Spirit and began to speak the word of God with boldness.

Teach by Example

The only way people will pray like this is if they are taught to pray like this. This means such prayer needs to be modeled by the pastor. He must show the people that prayer isn't just closing one's eyes and letting everything come out. Instead, prayer is careful, thoughtful, composed, articulated, and strategic—especially for public worship. First Timothy 2:1-4 is a great affirmation of this. Here, Paul instructed Timothy on how the church should function:

I urge that entreaties and prayers, petitions and thanksgivings, be made on behalf of all men, for kings and all who are in authority, so that we may lead a tranquil and quiet life in all godliness and dignity. This is good and acceptable in the sight of God our Savior, who desires all men to be saved and to come to the knowledge of the truth.

In this prescription, you have a clear diagnosis and even a recipe for what a pastor's congregational prayer should include. As well, this type of prayer keeps us from being self-focused and self-motivated.

Christians used to be known for their prayers, which were a major part of the service. Nowadays the prayer is just tacked on to the end of the sermon. Pastors no longer like to write conclusions and tend to end their sermons with, "Let's pray. God, grant us to live out the outline that I just preached." In contrast, church history is full of long and powerful prayers that have much variety. This is a helpful counterbalance to where most modern American evangelical churches are—the free prayer, because we think it's more spiritual to shoot from the hip than to plan in advance what you're going to say to God on behalf of your people. In *Lectures to My Sudents,* Spurgeon provides this counsel: "Let me, therefore, very earnestly caution you, beloved brethren, against spoiling your services by your prayers: make it your solemn resolve that all the engagements of the sanctuary shall be of the best kind."[11]

Corporate prayer…is a great reminder that we have congregational commitments and responsibilities to pray together and for one another.

Pastor MacArthur is a master of this, and I had the opportunity to ask him why he prays the way he does on a Sunday morning. He had a very simple answer: "I intend to lift up the people before God. I want to pray for them, with them, and on their behalf."[12] This is how we as pastors have to think about the role of pastoral prayer. Corporate prayer is the perfect antidote to the individualistic approach that is all too common today. It is a great reminder that we have congregational commitments and responsibilities to pray together and for one another.

Like it or not, every church has a liturgy. Perhaps you don't use the Book of Common Prayer, but even something as simple as welcoming the visitors, singing, and a sermon is a liturgy. And the question is, Are you doing all that God has intended for you to do in this gathered time of worship as Christians have been doing for thousands of years? The modern-day liturgy all too often looks like this: welcome, sing four songs, worship leader prays, sermon, concluding prayer, closing song, and everybody goes home. And that outline is absolutely historically impoverished, especially as it relates to prayer.

Types of Prayers

There are many kinds of prayers and a plethora of resources to help you develop variety in your corporate prayers. There are invocational prayers, which are intended to help the people cry out to God and call upon Him (Psalms 8; 100; 113). It is a profoundly biblical kind of prayer for starting a church service. A second kind of prayer is adoration and praise. This prayer recognizes God's greatness and grace. Third, there are prayers of confession, and you'll find these all through the Bible. These prayers simply acknowledge our sin and our need for grace. Usually they are done individually, but they ought to also be done corporately, as in Psalm 40:11-13 or 1 John 1:9: "If *we* confess our sins..." It makes sense for a pastor to pray, "Lord, we your people have sinned." You are not absolving them in some Roman Catholic ritual, but reminding them what God says about His grace—that there is full and free forgiveness in Christ.

The fourth type of prayer is a prayer of illumination. The apostle Paul prays this way in Ephesians 1:17-19. Fifth, you also need to have prayers of thanksgiving for all of God's good graces. Then sixth, along with prayers of thanksgiving, pastors need to pray prayers of intercession. The Reformers understood such prayers to include petitions for governing authorities, the welfare of the church (especially hurting individuals within it), and the progress of the gospel. Whenever Paul prayed for the progress of the gospel, he was offering up a prayer of intercession.

Pastoral Prayer: How to Do It Well

The *first* tip to better pastoral prayer is to prepare. Asking God for illumination is a wonderful place to start: "Open my eyes, that I may behold wonderful things from Your law" (Psalm 119:18). It is important to be thoughtful about what you're going to pray, to consider what the needs of the congregation are, and to be mindful of what your goal is in this prayer. This prayer does not necessarily need to be written out, but it's also not an extemporaneous prayer, for it's a prayer that you've thought about. It has been helpful for me to write down a brief list of points before I lead the church in prayer because I want to have a thoughtful structure to my prayer.

It's essential that we learn to differentiate between these kinds of prayers and our personal prayers. It's good to pray about circumstances, jobs, sickness, and events. Those things are naturally on everyone's mind. But we need to teach our people to pray bigger—to teach them to pray for wisdom, holiness, purity, and the advancement of the gospel. If you do not teach your people to pray like this, you'll have many earnest young men, worship leaders, and pastors default into their regular mode of prayer, which tends to be rote sentences that repeat the same catch phrases we are all familiar with. A practical way you can get prepared for a pastoral prayer is to pray Scripture.

A *second* tip is to not explain things to an omniscient God. This is a very common problem in corporate prayer. An example: "Lord, just as John Calvin once said a dog barks when his master is attacked, I would be a coward if I saw that God's truth is attacked and yet would remain silent." Are you telling God what John Calvin said? Should you put footnotes in your prayers?

Another example of this is what a good friend of mine, a pastor, prayed one Sunday morning: "Lord, your *ruach*, which means 'spirit...'" Afterward I asked him, "So you translate Hebrew for the Lord?" Your corporate prayer is intended to edify your people and even teach them how to pray. But remember that you are still talking to God, so stop telling Him what He already knows.

A *third* tip is to not preach or include announcements in your prayer. For example, inserting exhortations in your prayer can be awkward: "And Lord, help these hard-hearted people." You're talking to God, not preaching to your people. Spurgeon said, "Preach in the sermon and pray the prayer."[13] Nor is this the time to make announcements: "Lord, we pray that the junior high parents will get the deposits in by November 11 for the ski trip...At the men's ministry meeting, men whose last names start with A through J should bring donuts." Instead, use the time of prayer to consider God, His kingdom, and His people.

Make it your practice to pray well in public worship. It might be the best part. Spurgeon said, "Let your petitions be plain and heartfelt; and while you may sometimes feel that the sermon was below the mark, may they also feel that the prayer compensated for it all."[14]

Two Vital Components

The public reading of Scripture and corporate pastoral prayer can help transform a worship service. These two God-entranced and God-focused practices are not just a matter of getting rid of verbal tics or unnecessary lip smacks. Ultimately, we want to build our worship services to bring God honor and glory with excellence. We gather to worship God, and He has taught us how to worshop.

PRAYER

God, it is our desire to be equipped, to be thoughtful, to be engaged, and, ultimately, to hear from You. Father, may we grow in reverence for Your Word. Teach us to lead our people purposefully and to truly help them encounter You in worship. Thank You that we have access to You in prayer, and that this access reminds us of what Jesus accomplished at Calvary. Give us the courage to be men who lead your people in conviction, with humility, as You have directed us. May we please You in our lives, our ministries, and in the church. Amen.

FOSTERING FELLOWSHIP

"All the members of the body,
though they are many,
are one body, so also is Christ."

1 CORINTHIANS 12:12

12

Fostering Fellowship

John MacArthur
Shepherds' Conference 2014
1 Corinthians 12:12-27

Most pastors are familiar with the topic of church fellowship. Yet I want to take the opportunity here to raise your understanding of fellowship and your sense of responsibility for it, and to stress the urgency of implementing all of the elements of fellowship in the life of the church. With that in mind, we will examine 1 Corinthians 12:12-27.

> Even as the body is one and yet has many members, and all the members of the body, though they are many, are one body, so also is Christ. For by one Spirit we were all baptized into one body, whether Jews or Greeks, whether slaves or free, and we were all made to drink of one Spirit.
>
> For the body is not one member, but many. If the foot says, "Because I am not a hand, I am not a part of the body," it is not for this reason any the less a part of the body. And if the ear says, "Because I am not an eye, I am not a part of the body," it is not for this reason any the less a part of the body. If the whole body were an eye, where would the hearing be? If the whole were hearing, where would the sense of smell be? But now God has placed the members, each one of them, in the body, just as He desired. If they were all one member, where would the body

be? But now there are many members, but one body. And the eye cannot say to the hand, "I have no need of you"; or again the head to the feet, "I have no need of you." On the contrary, it is much truer that the members of the body which seem to be weaker are necessary; and those members of the body which we deem less honorable, on these we bestow more abundant honor, and our less presentable members become much more presentable, whereas our more presentable members have no need of it. But God has so composed the body, giving more abundant honor to that member which lacked, so that there may be no division in the body, but that the members may have the same care for one another. And if one member suffers, all the members suffer with it; if one member is honored, all the members rejoice with it.

Now you are Christ's body, and individually members of it.

The essence of church life is expressed graphically in the aforementioned metaphor. The life of the church is communal and is an intensely shared personal relationship with a spiritual thrust. This is what apostle Paul expressed in his extended metaphor of the body, and we find that truth repeated throughout the New Testament, particularly in Paul's epistles. For example, in Galatians 3, Paul emphasized that we are all one in Christ Jesus. In Ephesians 4:15-16, he wrote that we are all growing together to the fullness of the stature of Christ and that the Lord is fitting every part of the body together as one. In Philippians 2, Paul reminded us about caring for others more than ourselves, humbling ourselves, and having the attitude of Christ, which is selfless. This is what life in the church is to be like, and these passages re-establish in our minds the urgency of this matter of fellowship in the church.

The Blessing of Fellowship

Dietrich Bonhoeffer was very influential in my life, especially when I began pastoral ministry. His book *Life Together* had a profound impact on me. At that time I was studying the pastor's responsibility in developing fellowship in the church, and I was not able to find much on the topic.

While Bonhoeffer's book is not particularly theological—it's more devotional—I found it to be insightful and extremely helpful, particularly in light of how his life ended. On a gray dawn in April 1945, in a Nazi concentration camp at Flossenburg, Dietrich Bonhoeffer was executed by the order of Heinrich Himmler, who was Hitler's executioner. Bonhoeffer had been arrested about two years prior, and he was transferred from camp to camp: Tegel, Berlin, Buchenwald, Schoenberg, and Flossenburg.

During his transfers, Bonhoeffer lost all contact with the outside world. He became isolated from the people that he knew and loved. In fact, he was separated from all fellowship. And he had written *Life Together* a few years before that concentration camp experience. In that book, he wrote, "The physical presence of other Christians is a source of incomparable joy and strength to the believer. A physical sign of the gracious presence of the triune God, how inexhaustible are the riches that open up for those who, by God's will, are privileged to live in the daily fellowship of life with other Christians?"[1] He continued, "Let him who has such a privilege thank God on his knees and declare it is grace, nothing but grace that we are allowed to live in fellowship, in community with Christian brothers."[2] This man understood the blessing of enjoying fellowship with believers.

Jesus' Prayer for Fellowship

Multiple New Testament metaphors emphasize Christian fellowship. As Christ's church, we are bound to one husband. We are one set of branches connected to one vine. We are one flock with one shepherd, one kingdom with one king, one family with one father, and one building with one foundation. An even more intimate metaphor appears in 1 Corinthians 12—we are one body with one head. The metaphor of the body appears only in the New Testament, and thus is a unique way to understand the church.

Trinitarian fellowship is the model for fellowship in the church:
a shared life, shared love, shared purpose, shared truth,
and shared power. This is fellowship.

The church's fellowship is profound, spiritual, and real. It is a shared common life that is absolutely essential. It is what our Lord prayed for in His famous prayer in John 17, where He repeatedly said, "I pray that they may be one." Jesus was not praying for some kind of a social oneness, but for a spiritual reality. That prayer was answered when the church was born.

Jesus prayed that the Father would make His children one, just as He and the Father are one. What an amazing parallel! We are one in the way that the Son, the Father, and the Spirit are one. Trinitarian fellowship is the model for fellowship in the church: a shared life, shared love, shared purpose, shared truth, and shared power. This is fellowship.

In the New Testament, the Greek verb *koinoneo* is used eight times, and seven of those instances are translated "share," while in one instance it is translated "participates." The noun *koinonia* or *koinonos* appears about thirty times and has many different translations—"sharing," "contribution," "partnership," "participation," and sometimes "fellowship." The concept of fellowship then, refers to linking as partners and sharing a common life and cause. This is at the heart of life in the church, and this is what the church is.

Headed the Wrong Direction

It has been disturbing to witness in recent years that this has not been the direction the church has pursued. The church does not seem to be seeking a deeper, more profound expression of spiritual fellowship. Back in the 1980s, a Jewish humanist by the name of Neil Postman wrote a little book titled *Amusing Ourselves to Death*. Here is a Jewish humanist who is critiquing evangelical Christians and saying that they've lost their ability to think seriously because they are succumbing so much to entertainment. In the book he discusses the mind-crippling power of television, which does not engage people on an intellectual and meaningful level, but rather, causes them to sit like zombies and stare transfixed at a screen.

I do not think Neil Postman ever imagined that screens would consume so many American lives. The result has been devastating hyper-privacy. Screens are so private now that you can bring in the world of your own choosing through smartphones. Every person has become like a god, a creator of his own private universe, a secret world of preferences, downloading what he or she wants, eliminating what he or she does not want, and it has become a sphere of preferences and temptations. The smartphone is the most selfish necessity ever devised, and technology has put in our hands the most constant, the most accessible, the most visual private world of self-centered indulgence and temptation that humanity has ever known. You choose your music, your teachers, your entertainment, your friends, and like God, you become the creator of your world. The forest of temptations with which you can indulge yourself is devastating to fellowship.

Carl Trueman wrote on this topic, "The language of friendship is hijacked and cheapened by the Internet social networks, Facebook friends."[3] This is part of what some call the juvenilization of the church. Trueman continued, "The language of Facebook both reflects and encourages childishness. Childishness is a textually transmitted disease."[4] Research shows that the average high school student is on the Internet nine hours a day. Think about being a pastor and trying to create a fellowship with the next generation. Trueman wrote about the social media epidemic and said, "Such are human amoebas subsisting in a bizarre non-world that involves no risk to themselves, no giving of themselves to others, no true vulnerability, no commitment, no sacrifice, no real meaning or value. They are self-created avatars."[5]

Real fellowship does not exist in that digital world. Christianity is not a private experience; instead, privacy devastates the church. We are rapidly heading toward the norm of people creating their own virtual world and virtual self. I tweet, therefore I am. This is who I am—the perfect, indomitable me, self-actualized like some technologically created science-of-mind projection.

Tragically, the culture is becoming more isolated, consumeristic, and self-absorbed. Consequently, developing fellowship is very difficult. Sadly, the evangelical church for decades has been trying to give the culture what it wants—privacy, convenience, and no accountability. The culture wants fellowship to die, and church life is falling victim to this seductive design.

Even attendance in many megachurches is on the decline because the trend is for people to belong to the first church of iTunes. One of the largest churches in America is an online church. I read an advertisement by a church that proclaimed, "Join an e-group." This is the trend, because at a real church you might have to face someone you don't agree with. At a real church you might have to sit next to somebody you're not too fond of. At a real church you might hear a message from a preacher who doesn't say what you want to hear. Worst of all, you might have to sing an old hymn in 4/4 time led by a senior citizen. Can you imagine the horror? That would be way too much for those who prefer an individualistic self-created world. For many, all information, all experience, and all relationships are based upon their own defined entitlement. That rules out truth, accuracy, credibility, rationality, sacrifice, deferred gratification, and meaningful relationships.

This is illustrated in a *Christianity Today* article by Kevin Miller. He wrote about Donald Miller, Rob Bell, and Brian McLaren all leaving the church. Ironically, ten years ago they were considered the most influential evangelicals in the world. These leaders were part of the Emergent Church movement that imploded because of personalized entitlement religion. They had a bias against the accuracy, authority, and clarity of the Word of God. They formed a personalized religion that collapsed when people began to realize that there was no reason to get together. Donald Miller says on his blog, "I don't connect with God by singing to Him." He poses the question, "So do I attend church? Not often, to be honest."[6] In another instance he discusses having communion along the side of the road with chocolate chip cookies and cocoa. The idea is to create your own sacraments and your own hyper-individualized faith.

The sad reality is that in the last 20 years, the church has succumbed to a weak ecclesiology. Even in the midst of a revival of reformed theology, we are losing a whole generation to individualistic antifellowship habits. Even as a pastor, you feel pressure when someone asks, "What are you doing in your church with technology? What are you doing with social media?" Like most other things, technology has its value and can be a tool for good, but it is also an outlet for disastrous evil. As leaders, we cannot let the cyberspace replace real fellowship. Everything about the church fights against privacy, isolation, and narcissism.

What We Need to Know About Fellowship
The Basis of Fellowship

To help correct the church's errant trajectory, we have to understand the basis of fellowship. First John 1:1 is probably the most definitive verse on the basis of fellowship: "What was from the beginning, what we have heard, what we have seen with our eyes, what we have looked at and touched with our hands concerning the Word of Life…" John was writing about his firsthand experience with the incarnate God in Christ. He went on to say, "The life was manifested, and we've seen and testify and proclaim to you the eternal life, which was with the Father and was manifested to us—what we have seen and heard we proclaim to you also, so that you too may have fellowship with us; and indeed our fellowship is with the Father, and with His Son Jesus Christ" (verses 2-3).

The goal of the gospel is not just individual salvation for people who then are privileged to do what they want, but rather, to create a fellowship.

The basis of fellowship is the word of salvation. The proclamation of the gospel was so that "you too may have fellowship with us, and indeed our fellowship is with the Father, and with His Son." John was stressing that the proclamation of the gospel has a goal in mind: to create a partnership, a shared life, a shared purpose, a shared power, and a shared ministry. The goal of the gospel is not just individual salvation for people who then are privileged to do what they want, but rather, to create a fellowship. This is what Jesus prayed for, and here John wrote about the answer to Jesus' prayer.

When Jesus was praying that His followers become one, He wasn't talking about some kind of social unity; He was praying about a real unity that is fulfilled in the work of the Spirit of God, who comes and creates the body of Christ by His own indwelling. In 1 Corinthians 6:17 Paul wrote, "The one who joins himself to the Lord is one spirit with Him." Therefore he who is one with the Lord is one with all those who are the Lord's.

It is common to hear people say, "This member or that member is out of fellowship." Yet that's not accurate because if you are out of fellowship, you are an unbeliever. For if you are a believer, then you are in fellowship, because the basis of that fellowship is salvation. As a result, that puts all believers in union with each other. Every saved person is then mandated and entitled to full involvement in that fellowship. Our responsibility extends to others, for God has put our lives together for spiritual purposes.

After John makes it clear that the basis of fellowship is salvation, he draws a contrast in 1 John 1:5-7:

> This is the message we have heard from Him and announce to you, that God is Light, and in Him there is no darkness at all. If we say that we have fellowship with Him and yet walk in the darkness, we lie and do not practice the truth; but if we walk in the Light as He Himself is in the Light, we have fellowship with one another, and the blood of Jesus His Son cleanses us from all sin.

An individual is either in the light or in the darkness, either saved or lost, either in fellowship or out of it. Believers are always in the fellowship, for they are in the light.

One wants to be careful about saying that another person is out of fellowship. Some may experience a time of wandering like David did, during which he said, "Restore to me the joy of Your salvation" (Psalm 51:12). Or as Donald Grey Barnhouse used to say, "There is a great difference between falling down on the deck of a ship, and falling overboard."[7] If you are on the deck of fellowship, though you may stumble and fall into sin—in fact, you will sin (1:8-10)—that is not fatal because, as 1 John 2:1 says, "If anyone sins, we have an Advocate with the Father, Jesus Christ the righteous; and He Himself is the propitiation for our sins; and not for ours only, but also for those of the whole world." We may fall on the deck, but that's not terminal, for the fellowship of the believers is forever.

Bonhoeffer wrote,

> I am a brother to another person through what Jesus Christ did for me and to me. The other person has become a brother to

me through what Jesus Christ did for Him. This fact that we are brothers only through Jesus Christ is of an immeasurable significance. It is not what a man is, he writes in himself, as a Christian, his spirituality and piety, that's not the basis of our fellowship. What determines our fellowship is what that man is, by reason, of Christ. Our fellowship with one another consists solely in what Christ has done in both of us. It remains so for time and eternity.[8]

Moreover, he wrote, "Christian fellowship is not an ideal which we must achieve. It is a reality created by God in Christ." Again, salvation is the basis of fellowship.

The Nature of Fellowship

After we've established that salvation is the basis of fellowship, it is necessary to examine the nature of fellowship. In Acts 2, Peter preached a powerful sermon, and 3000 souls were added to the church by receiving the Word and being baptized (verse 41). These believers then continually devoted themselves to the apostles' teaching, fellowship, the breaking of bread, and prayer (2:42). Even beyond that,

all those who had believed were together and had all things in common; and they began selling their property and possessions and were sharing them with all, as anyone might have need. Day by day continuing with one mind in the temple, and breaking bread from house to house, they were taking their meals together with gladness and sincerity of heart, praising God and having favor with all the people. And the Lord was adding to their number day by day those who were being saved (verses 44-47).

The reality of fellowship is togetherness and sharing—sharing in a spiritual way as well as in a temporal way. We are told that the early church continually devoted themselves to all these things collectively. They expressed their partnership and spiritual union even in temporal ways. History reveals that many people were converted in that great event, and subsequent to that, lingered in Jerusalem because it was the only church in the world. They had come from the Diaspora back for the events of Passover and Pentecost. And since this was the only church at the time, they stayed, were cared for, and had their needs met.

That is why people began selling their property and possessions, "and we're sharing them with all, as anyone might have need" (verse 45). The verb tense of the Greek word translated "selling" is imperfect, which means they began continually sharing their resources. They gave to such an extent that they sold and liquidated their property to provide for each other. The impact of this is evident in verse 47: They were "having favor with all the people. And the Lord was adding to their number day by day those who were being saved." A church with genuine, sacrificial, and loving fellowship is a powerful testimony to the world. In John 13:35, Jesus said, "All men will know that you are My disciples, if you have love for one another." This is not a reference to the emotion of love, but the expression of it. That is fellowship.

Aristides, a pagan looking at Christians, wrote the famous statement, "They abstain from all impurity in the hope of the reckonings that is to come in another world. When there is among them a man that is poor and needy, and if they have not abandons of necessities, they fast two or three days that they may supply the needy with the necessary food, such is the law of the Christians and such is their conduct."[9] The church is to be a powerful testimony to the world. Yet in today's context that is being lost, particularly with the prosperity gospel, which feeds the selfishness and childishness of the so-called "church." The testimony of the church must stay intact, but privacy and solitude are hindrances to that.

The Symbol of Fellowship

Next, I want to look at the symbol of fellowship, which we read about in 1 Corinthians 10:16-17: "Is not the cup of blessing which we bless a sharing in the blood of Christ? Is not the bread which we break a sharing in the body of Christ? Since there is one bread, we who are many are one body; for we all partake of the one bread." The symbol of fellowship is the Lord's Table. This is where we all end up on our knees at the foot of the cross. This is the leveler where there is neither Jew nor Greek, male nor female, bond nor free. It is a magnificent symbol of our common shared life grounded in Christ's atoning work.

As the pastor of Grace Community Church, one of the things I have tried to do through the years is emphasize that communion is looking back at the cross, but it also presently looks at the body of Christ as one group of sinners who together are humbled on their knees before the sacrifice of the Son of God. The church body has a common partnership in salvation. However, this truth is being diminished. Once when I was out of town I visited a large and well-known church, and it was a painful experience. At the end of his gross mishandling of Scripture, the pastor said, "This is communion Sunday. There is some bread and juice by the exits. Just grab some on your way out." I endured up to that point, but could no longer bear it, for treating the Lord's Table in that manner is abominable.

Though there is no prescription in the Scripture as to how often we are to partake in the Lord's Table, whenever we do, we are to be looking at the cross in deep and honest self-examination, and we should also stress the fellowship aspect of the ordinance. The church is all one body of people who are equally unworthy, equally graced with eternal life. We are all equally redeemed by Christ, and we are all equally bearing eternal life from Him and sustained in Him. The Lord's Table humbles us, levels us, and calls us to serious self-examination. But it also vividly celebrates our union with each other. Make much of the Lord's Table and treat it seriously, not casually.

The Danger to Fellowship

Fourth, we must be warned of the danger to fellowship, which is sin. Sin not only brings discipline on the believer, but it devastates the fellowship, shatters the unity, restricts the ministry, holds back the power, and confuses the purpose. That is why in 1 Corinthians 11:27 we read, "Whoever eats the bread or drinks the cup of the Lord in an unworthy manner, shall be guilty of the body and the blood of the Lord." Sinful habits and lack of proper self-examination are so serious that the Lord may make people sick and some of them may end up dying. In verse 31 Paul reinforced this: "If we judged ourselves rightly, we would not be judged." The rationale behind this is found in 1 Corinthians 5:6: "A little leaven leavens the whole lump of dough." As pastors, we are called to shut people out of partaking in the symbol if they are unwilling to confess all their sin. Individuals who do not take this seriously do not understand the significance of the unity of the church.

Matthew 18 contains the first instruction in the New Testament that mentions the church, and here is the charge:

> If your brother sins, go and show him his fault in private; if he listens to you, you have won your brother. But if he does not listen to you, take one or two more with you, so that by the mouth of two or three witnesses every fact may be confirmed. If he refuses to listen to them, tell it to the church; and if he refuses to listen even to the church, let him be to you as a Gentile and a tax collector (verses 15-17).

I'm convinced that the future of the church does not depend on cultural relevance, or marketing, or technology. Rather, the future of the church depends on the church's holiness. For the sake of fellowship, you must deal with sin in the church.

Note what Paul wrote in 2 Corinthians 12:15 when he was brokenhearted by the way the church in Corinth had treated him: "I would most gladly spend and be expended for your souls." Paul would have given his life for the spiritual well-being of the Corinthians. He then said,

> All this time you have been thinking that we are defending ourselves to you. Actually, it is in the sight of God that we have been speaking in Christ; and all for your upbuilding, beloved. For I am afraid that perhaps when I come I may find you to be not what I wish and may be found by you to be not what you wish; that perhaps there will be strife, jealousy, angry tempers, disputes, slanders, gossip, arrogance, disturbances; I am afraid that when I come again my God may humiliate me before you, and I may mourn over many of those who have sinned in the past and not repented of the impurity, immorality and sensuality which they have practiced (verses 19-21).

Paul was burdened about the purity of the church. The same should be true of you as a pastor. This is the hard work of the ministry. The future of your ministry corresponds directly to your passion for the truth and the holiness of your church. Media cleverness may get crowds, but it does not produce holiness. But holiness does bring Jesus Christ to church, because where two or three are gathered together in a discipline situation, Christ is there in your midst. Sin endangers pure fellowship, so prevent the privacy of sin.

The Duty of Fellowship

Up to now we have seen that the basis of fellowship is salvation. The nature of fellowship is a shared life, both spiritual and temporal. The symbol of fellowship is the Lord's Table. And the danger to fellowship is sin. Fifth, we must understand the duty of fellowship.

In Matthew 18, we see the negative aspect of the duty of fellowship: "Whoever causes one of these little ones who believe in Me to stumble"— that is, sin—"it would be better for him to have a heavy millstone hung around his neck and be drowned in the depth of the sea" (verse 6). It would be better off for you to drown with a millstone around your neck than to cause a fellow Christian to stumble. In verse 7 Jesus continued, "Woe to the world because of its stumbling blocks!" In verse 10 He said, "See that you do not despise one of these little ones." The principle is prescribed from a negative standpoint: Do not lead another believer into sin.

Someone can cause other believers to stumble by flaunting a liberty, despising them, belittling them, withholding what they need from them, ridiculing them, treating them with indifference, defrauding them, taking advantage of them, or even by failing to confront their sinfulness. Then note the contrasting positive statement in verse 5: "Whoever receives one such child in My name receives Me." When you welcome another believer into your life, no matter who that believer is, you're receiving Christ. Positively, you want to receive other believers; negatively, you don't want to offend other believers. That's the pattern that is required of you, for that is the duty of fellowship.

There are a few reasons given in Matthew 18 for why we should not offend fellow Christians. First, because of the relationship that believers have to angels: "See that you do not despise one of these little ones, for I say to you that their angels in heaven continually see the face of My Father who is in heaven" (verse 10). That's an amazing statement reminiscent of the custom in Eastern courts, in which highly respected men chose servants who would stand on their behalf before the king and look into the king's face. We know, according to Hebrews 1:14, that angels minister to the saints—they watch, guide, provide, protect, deliver, dispatch answers to prayer, and do more for all who belong to God. Therefore, we ought to be careful how we treat other believers because the angels are watching.

Second, we want to treat other Christians with care because of Christ. Jesus said, "Whoever receives one such child in My name receives Me" (Matthew 18:5).

Third, fellowship reflects your relationship to God. Matthew wrote,

> What do you think? If any man has a hundred sheep, and one of them has gone astray, does he not leave the ninety-nine on the mountains and go and search for the one that is straying? If it turns out that he finds it, truly I say to you, he rejoices over it more than over the ninety-nine which have not gone astray. So it is not the will of your Father who is in heaven that one of these little ones perish (18:12-14).

We care for one another in the body of Christ by making sure we receive other believers as we would receive Christ, and by never having a negative influence and leading another believer into temptation or sin. Our duty in fellowship is to be an instrument of holiness in the lives of other believers, which embraces the "one anothers" of the New Testament. Christian fellowship consists of confessing your sins one to another, forgiving one another, loving one another, exhorting one another, edifying one another, teaching one another, admonishing one another, and praying for one another. That is fellowship, and it is personal because it militates against privacy, isolation, narcissism, and self-centeredness.

The Result of Fellowship

The result of this kind of fellowship is simply stated in 1 John 1:3-4: "What we have seen and heard we proclaim to you also, so that you too may have fellowship with us; and indeed our fellowship is with the Father, and with His Son Jesus Christ. These things we write, so that our joy may be made complete." When biblical fellowship is understood and cultivated, the result is joy. Where you have a congregation of people pursuing the realities of fellowship, you have a manifestation of joy that transcends all the pains of life and comes out of shared sacrifice and meaningful spiritual relationships. I can testify that the joy in my own life and the joy in our church is the product of living in the fullness of fellowship.

PRAYER

Lord, it is appropriate for us to consider what the apostle Paul wrote: "Finally, brethren, rejoice, be made complete, be comforted, be like-minded, live in peace; and the God of love and peace will be with you. Greet one another with a holy kiss. All the saints greet you. The grace of the Lord Jesus Christ, and the love of God, and the fellowship of the Holy Spirit, be with you all" (2 Corinthians 13:11-14). That's our benediction. May it be so, in Jesus' name, Amen.

Notes

Chapter 2—Purity in the Camp (Ligon Duncan)

1. Geoffrey J. Martin, *American Geography and Geographies: Toward Geographical Science* (New York: Oxford University Press, 2015), 864.

Chapter 3—Hallowed Be Your Name (Tom Pennington)

1. Thomas Watson, *The Lord's Prayer* (http://www.ccel.org/ccel/watson/prayer.txt), 516.

2. Don Whitney, *Spiritual Disciplines of the Christian Life* (Colorado Springs: NavPress, 1991), 62.

3. Augustine, Letters, "Letter to Proba," Letter 130.

4. Augustine, "Sermons to Brothers in the Desert."

5. Whitney, *Spiritual Disciplines*, 64.

6. John Calvin, *Institutes of the Christian Religion* (Philadelphia, PA: Westminster, 1960), 850.

7. Calvin, *Institutes*, 853.

8. John Owen, "Sermon II: A Memorial of the Deliverance of Essex County, and Committee," on Habakkuk 3:1-9.

9. Jonathan Edwards, *The Works of Jonathan Edwards* (Peabody, MA: Hendrickson, 2003) v. 2, 455.

10. Quoted in Richard Baxter, *The Reformed Pastor* (Portland, OR: Multnomah, 1982), 17.

11. Baxter, *The Reformed Pastor*, 18.

12. John Calvin, *Calvin's Commentaries*, vol. XVI (Grand Rapids, MI: Baker, 2005), 328.

13. J.C. Ryle, *A Call to Prayer* (Grand Rapids, MI: Baker, 1979), 35.

14. John Owen, Kelly Kapic, and Justin Taylor, *Overcoming Sin and Temptation* (Wheaton, IL: Crossway, 2006), 86-88.

15. See http://www.nielsen.com/us/en/insights/news/2012/the-cross-platform-report-how-and-where -content-is-watched.html.

16. As cited in John Piper, *Brothers, We Are Not Professionals* (Nashville, TN: Broadman & Holman, 2002), 63.

17. Calvin, *Institutes*, 917.

18. John Watkins, *The Sermons of...Hugh Latimer* (London: J. Duncan, 1824), 2.

Chapter 4—A Leader Who Suffers Well

1. Marvin Vincent, *Epistle to the Philippians and to Philemon* (Edinburgh: T. & T. Clark, 1897), 78.

2. Martin Luther, *"A Mighty Fortress Is Our God."*

Chapter 7—The Leader and His Flock (Rick Holland)

1. Thomas Schreiner, *The New American Commentary, 1, 2 Peter, Jude* (Nashville, TN: Broadman & Holman, 2003), 232.

2. As cited in Larry J. Michael, *Spurgeon on Spiritual Leadership* (Grand Rapids, MI: Kregel, 2003), 153.

3. Michael, *Spurgeon.*

4. Michael, *Spurgeon*, 154.

5. Richard Baxter, *The Reformed Pastor,* 4th ed. (Glasgow: Oliver & Boyd, Wm. Whyte & Co., and Wm. Oliphant, 1835), 181.

Chapter 8—Guarding the Gospel (Steven J. Lawson)

1. David A. Lopez, *Separatist Christianity: Spirit and Matter in the Early Church Fathers* (Baltimore, MD: The Johns Hopkins University Press, 2004), 83.

2. John Phillips, *Exploring Proverbs: An Expository Commentary,* vol. 1 (Neptune, NJ: Loizeaux Brothers, 1995), 286.

3. J.C. Ryle, *A Sketch of the Life and Labors of George Whitefield* (New York: Anson D.F. Randolph, 1854), 29.

4. See http://www.cnn.com/TRANSCRIPTS/0506/20/lkl.01.html.

5. See http://www.cnn.com/TRANSCRIPTS/0506/20/lkl.01.html.

6. J.C. Ryle, *Simplicity in Preaching* (http://gracegems.org/18/Ryle-%20Preaching.htm).

7. Martin Luther, *What Luther Says*, vol. 2, 702-4, 715.

8. Luther, *What Luther Says.*

9. Martin Luther, *Luther's Works*, 26. 55.

10. James Montgomery Boice, "Galatians," *Expositor's Bible Commentary,* vol. 10 (Grand Rapids, MI: Zondervan, 1976) 429.

11. John Knox, *The History of the Reformation of Religion in Scotland* (Edinburgh: Banner of Truth, 1982), 250; Joseph Adolphe Petit, *History of Mary Stuart: Queen of Scots* (London: Longman, Green), 244.

12. John Knox, *The Works of John Knox,* vol. 6, liii.

13. Scots Confession of 1560.

Chapter 9—No Little People, No Little Sermons (Albert Mohler Jr.)

1. John Calvin, *The Gospel According to John 1–10* (Grand Rapids, MI: Eerdmans, 1995), 237.

2. Calvin, *The Gospel According to John 1–10.*

3. Calvin, *The Gospel According to John 1–10*, 237-38.

Chapter 11—What Is Missing from Your Church Service? (Austin Duncan)

1. Jeff Kirkland, *An Historical, Biblical, and Practical Analysis of Public Scripture Reading in Corporate Worship Gatherings* (Sun Valley, CA: The Master's Seminary), 2.

2. Everett Ferguson, *Early Christians Speak* (Abilene, TX: Biblical Research Press, 1981), 86.

3. Philip H. Towner, *The Function of the Public Reading of Scripture in 1 Timothy 4:13 and in the Biblical Tradition* (http://www.sbts.edu/wpcontent/uploads/sites/5/2010/07/sbjt_073_fall03_towner1.pdf), 53.

4. Mark Earey, "This Is the Word of the Lord: The Bible and Worship," *Anvil 19*, no. 2 (2002): 92.

5. David F. Wells, *God in the Wasteland* (Grand Rapids, MI: Eerdmans, 1994), 150.

6. Ferguson, *Early Christians Speak*, 87.

7. Jeffery D. Arthurs, *Devote Yourself to the Public Reading of Scripture* (Grand Rapids, MI: Kregel, 2012), 14.

8. Stephen Olford, "Why I Believe in Expository Preaching," audiotape of pastors' luncheon message at Dauphin Way Baptist Church, Mobile, Alabama, March 22, 1999.

9. Bryan Chapell, "The Incarnate Voice: An Exhortation for Excellence in the Oral Reading of Scripture,", *Presbyterion* vol. 15, no 1 (Spring 1989(, 42-57, 42-43.

10. Allen Ross, *Recalling the Hope of Glory* (Grand Rapids, MI: Kregel Academic, 2006), 506.

11. C.H. Spurgeon, *Lectures to My Students,* First Series (New York: Sheldon and Company, 1875), 85.

12. A collection of John MacArthur's pulpit prayers have been compiled in the book *A Year of Prayer* (Eugene, OR: Harvest House, 2011).

13. Spurgeon, Lectures to My Students, 92.

14. Helmut Thielicke, *Encounter with Spurgeon* (Cambridge: James Clark, 1964), 135.

Chapter 12—Fostering Fellowship (John MacArthur)

1. Dietrich Bonhoeffer, *Life Together: Prayerbook of the Bible* (Minneapolis, MN: Fortress, 2004), 29.

2. Ibid., 30.

3. See http://www.reformation21.org/counterpoints/wages-of-spin/no-text-please-im-british.php.

4. See http://www.reformation21.org/counterpoints/wages-of-spin/no-text-please-im-british.php.

5. See http://www.reformation21.org/counterpoints/wages-of-spin/no-text-please-im-british.php.

6. Donald Miller, http://storylineblog.com/2014/02/03/i-dont-worship-god-by-singing-i-connect-with-him-elsewhere/.

7. Donald Grey Barnhouse, *Your Questions Answered from the Bible* (Philadelphia, PA: The Evangelical Foundation, 1957), 29.

8. Bonhoeffer, *Life Together*, 25.

9. The Apology of Aristides, *Syriac text and translation*. Cited in *Encyclopedia Britannica*, vol. 1 (Chicago: Encyclopedia Britannica), 346.

CONTRIBUTORS

John MacArthur is pastor-teacher of Grace Community Church in Sun Valley, California, and president of The Master's College and Seminary.

Ligon Duncan is the chancellor/CEO of Reformed Theological Seminary and the John E. Richards Professor of Systematic and Historical Theology.

Tom Pennington is the pastor-teacher of Countryside Bible Church in Southlake, Texas.

John Piper is the chancellor of Bethlehem College & Seminary, Minneapolis, Minnesota. He ministered at Bethlehem Baptist Church for 33 years and now travels to speak, and writes regularly, through Desiring God.

Mark Dever is senior pastor of Capitol Hill Baptist Church in Washington, DC, and the president of 9Marks.

Rick Holland is the senior pastor of Mission Road Bible Church in Prairie Village, Kansas.

Steven J. Lawson is president of OnePassion Ministries and a professor of preaching at The Master's Seminary and at The Ligonier Academy.

Albert Mohler Jr. is president of the Southern Baptist Theological Seminary in Louisville, Kentucky.

Austin T. Duncan is the college pastor at Grace Community Church in Sun Valley, California. He also oversees the preaching curriculum and the DMin program at the Master's Seminary.

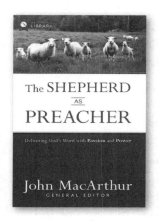

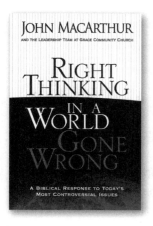
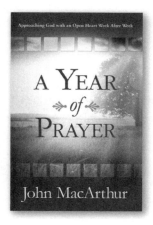

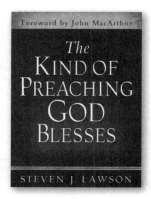

The Kind of Preaching God Blesses

Steven J. Lawson

Real power in preaching—that is, the power that brings true revival and transforms lives—comes from God alone. That is why it is so essential to follow the pattern for preaching given in Scripture—a pattern found in 1 Corinthians 2:1-9. Fulfill your high calling in ministry as you come to understand the priority of biblical preaching, the poverty of modern preaching, and the power of the Spirit in preaching.

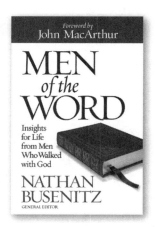

Men of the Word

Nathan Busenitz, General Editor

What is God's calling for men? What character qualities does He value? What is biblical manhood, and how is it cultivated? You'll find the answers to these all-important questions in the lives of the men of the Bible—men like Abraham, David, Nehemiah, and Paul. Every one of them struggled with the same issues men like you face today. From them you'll learn how to live by faith, lead with courage, pray with boldness, flee temptation, find satisfaction in God, and more.

To learn more about Harvest House books and
to read sample chapters, visit our website:

www.harvesthousepublishers.com

HARVEST HOUSE PUBLISHERS
EUGENE, OREGON